SHADE IT BLACK

(Photo courtesy of Edward Kaspar)

Shade It Black
Death and After in Iraq

Jess Goodell

with

John Hearn

CASEMATE

Philadelphia & Newbury

Published in the United States of America and Great Britain in 2011 by
CASEMATE PUBLISHERS
908 Darby Road, Havertown, PA 19083
and
17 Cheap Street, Newbury RG14 5DD

Copyright 2011 © Jess Goodell and John Hearn

ISBN 978-1-61200-001-5
Digital Edition: ISBN 978-1-61200-012-1

Cataloging-in-publication data is available from the Library of Congress
and the British Library.

10 9 8 7 6 5 4 3 2 1

Printed and bound in the United States of America.

For a complete list of Casemate titles please contact:

CASEMATE PUBLISHERS (US)
Telephone (610) 853-9131, Fax (610) 853-9146
E-mail: casemate@casematepublishing.com

CASEMATE PUBLISHERS (UK)
Telephone (01635) 231091, Fax (01635) 41619
E-mail: casemate-uk@casematepublishing.co.uk

Table of Contents

Contents (cont'd)

To the Marines of the Mortuary Affairs Platoon, Camp Al Taqaddum, Iraq, 2004: I told this story to the best of my ability. I tried to tell it as accurately and as honestly as possible. I know that you sheltered me from the greatest threats and shielded me from the most horrific tasks, even though it meant a greater burden for you. That sacrifice, of which I am always aware, has helped me to experience a depth of meaning that I did not know existed. Semper Fi!

Mortuary Affairs bunker in Camp Al Taqaddum, Iraq, on the right. Tent city, where many Marines slept and lived, is along the horizon. (Author collection)

Tell me the last time you saw the body of a dead American soldier. What does that look like? Who in America knows what that looks like? Because I know what that looks like, and I feel responsible for the fact that no one else does . . .

—Lara Logan,
CBS's Chief Foreign Correspondent, 2008

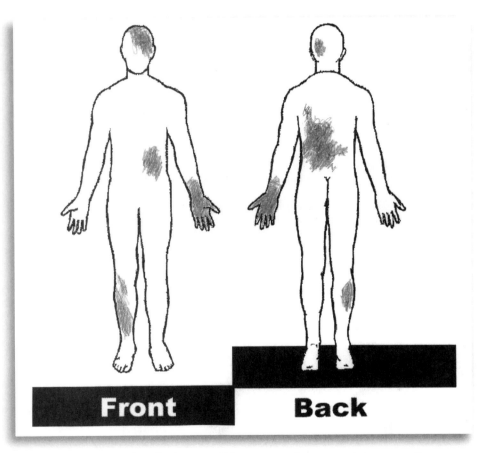

Front **Back**

Diagram used to shade areas of the remains that were missing, as well as to indicate tattoos and other identifying marks. (Author collection)

Prologue

THE BILL

Wars are not paid for in wartime, the bill comes later.
—Benjamin Franklin

Every day for months on end a man in his early twenties, wearing clothes several sizes too big for him, wanders through downtown Baton Rouge. He is looking for something he lost. An emaciated woman, also in her early twenties, sits alone in a Tucson apartment she's been unable to leave for three months. If she could bring herself to leave, she would see a psychologist. A skinny, chronically jobless kid in Oregon is high this afternoon, as always. A thirty-three-year-old living near Boston is arrested for having shot at neighborhood teens through his apartment window. He told police he was afraid they were about to attack his family. Another young man sits in a wheelchair in an Ohio hospital, unable to use his legs after injecting them with drugs in a failed suicide attempt. He texts this message, "I have $2,000 in the bank. Let's meet in NYC and go out with a bang."

Most explosions and most deaths occurred on and around bridges.
The insurgents hid on top or underneath them and watched
as we approached. (Photo courtesy of David Leeson)

1

To Iraq

WASHINGTON—*Word was already circulating throughout Washington that the Marines were planning operational changes in Iraq. Without criticizing the Army's heavy-handed tactics on the ground there, the Marines were quietly working on changing operational tactics.*

During the Iraq War, I got to know some of their tactics. Their orders from their commanders were to "win the hearts and the minds of the Iraqi people." They were tough when they had to be, but also thoughtful and considerate.

But now, as they prepare to relieve the Army in some parts of Iraq, the Marines are formulating new ways to interact with civilians, using restraint in the use of force and emphasizing cultural sensitivity.

Marine commanders, recognize the Iraqi population is angered by current military tactics such as knocking down doors of houses and shops, demolishing buildings, flattening fruit orchards, firing artillery in civilian areas and isolating entire neighborhoods with barbed wire fences...

According to an internal Marine document,

*platoons of Marines soon to arrive in Iraq intend to
live among Iraqis in their towns and villages while
training the Iraqi police and civil defense forces.
These units will resemble an armed version of the
Peace Corps, and will be fully informed about Iraqi
culture, customs and Islamic traditions.*

From: "Preparing Marines for Iraq,"
by Barbara Ferguson, *The Arab News*, March 27, 2004

We walked up the ramp of a huge transport plane whose back end opened like a Thanksgiving turkey. Our destination: Kuwait, soon followed by Iraq. We were packed into its fuselage as though we were stuffing, sitting shoulder to shoulder, with the entire side of the body of one person touching the entire side of the body of the next, from shoulders to feet. Identical and attached, we resembled one of those paper people chains that grade school students make. Our knees were touching the knees of the person facing us, so we were boxed in on three sides by strangers. Many of us were wearing earplugs, but even if we had not been, the plane was too loud for conversation and, as Marines, we could not voice our innate human fear. For the eighteen-hour flight, we sat there, against each other, letting our thoughts wander.

When we landed in Kuwait, many of us already had our war face on. Our weapons were on "condition 3," "magazine inserted, chamber empty, bolt forward, safety on, ejection port cover on." We were on the lookout—because here we were, finally, in the Middle East. Young men who worked out every day puffed out their chests and positioned their arms in ways that made their biceps bulge. Smaller men held their M-16s in the same way they had seen Rambo hold his weapon in long ago movies. The Hispanic and Black kids assumed threatening facial expressions and thugged-up their gait, taking up as much space as possible when they rolled by. The White guys clenched their jaws and narrowed their eyes. Every Marine's head swiveled continuously, their eyes searching the environment for threats.

In Kuwait, we had to wait for the vehicles—the Humvees and the seven tons as well as the heavy equipment, the wratches and trams—to arrive before we could set up for the convoy. During the three or so week stay in Kuwait, we trained. A favorite session had us standing in the desert sand in the spots we would have been in had we actually been in real vehicles. I would pretend I was behind the wheel of a Humvee while Copas stood to my right, a foot or so away. Five other Marines positioned themselves behind us, where they would sit . . . as if we were in a vehicle. At random times, Sergeant Johnson would shout out, "Ambush, right!" and we would all dive into the sand, forming a perimeter. Then we would practice advancing while attacking maneuvers by springing up and lunging forward and back down into the sand. "I'm up, they see me, I'm down," we would repeat to ourselves. For a moment or two it might have seemed like a joke, especially when we were riding along in our invisible Humvee, but at the same time, we each knew that it was possible that in a day or two we would be ambushed and would have to know what to do.

When the vehicles arrived, the Mortuary Affairs platoon was fortunate enough to have been assigned three Humvees and a seven ton and because I had my Humvee license and was a mechanic, I was assigned to drive one of them. Copas was my A driver—my assistant driver—and was in the front passenger seat. Our unarmored vehicle—our doors were about two inches thick whereas the Army had steel and Kevlar reinforced six inch doors— was open in the back where there were two benches that seated the other five Marines. It is difficult for the driver to wield a weapon, so my M-16 was propped upright, wedged against the door. The Marines in the back of the Humvee provided security.

We left at 3:00 a.m. and drove until 11:00 p.m. that night, when we pulled into an Army detachment base, which was more of a checkpoint, one of several that could be found along a major route, in order for convoys to refuel or sleep. We parked our vehicles where they would need to be in the morning, positioned for a rapid exit in the event we were attacked and had to leave quickly. The army set up a perimeter and stood post while we tried our best to change our socks, use the head, brush our teeth, eat something, and find a place to sleep. Many of the men jostled around trying to find a warm spot on the hood of a truck, high above the sand. People crashed in the backs of the Humvees or on top of the seven tons, anywhere they could find space. By the time we might have begun to calm down but before we were able to sleep, it was time to go. On paper we got four hours of sleep, but in reality, on the ground, there in Iraq, we got none.

We drove from 0300 to 2300 for three nights. We stopped at various Army checkpoints to take advantage of their perimeters. Sometimes we traveled along a sort of highway, with street lamps along its edges, but nothing else, nothing that could be seen on either side of the road, just the highway itself.

One afternoon we were beat from the tension and the lack of sleep. There was nothing but sand as far as we could see in every direction, except for the paved road we were on, when I looked up ahead and noticed a man, walking. One man walking, alone, in the middle of nothing, like a solitary man on the moon. It didn't make sense. I was tired and the situation was tense and the vast and monotonous sameness of the scenery made me wonder if I were hallucinating. I couldn't imagine where he was coming from or where he was going. *Where is this guy going? What is he doing?* There was nothing at all around. Occasionally we would see a home on the side of the road made from clay and grass or straw. One solitary house, alone, on a barren moonscape, like the man I saw. A tiny, little one-room house. I thought, *"What's this house doing here? Is it really here?"* There was nothing else as far as you could see. There was nothing.

The next day, a week day, we drove through a village, and saw several young children running around. *Why aren't they in school? What are you little ones doing running around in the streets? Is it because we are here?* Outside the villages, the convoy would pull just to the side of the road for a break and that was when all the guys would form a long straight line, all facing in the same direction, and urinate into the sand. Some of the female Marines chose not to relieve themselves. They must have regulated their water intake and sweated most of it out because very few seemed to go when they had this chance.

On the third day the convoy came to an abrupt halt. We may have been attacked or maybe there was a firefight up ahead, but the line of vehicles was so long and we were so far back that it was impossible to say. We pulled off to the side of the road, jumped from our vehicles and hid in the dirt and grass of the embankment to provide a perimeter for the convoy. Were we under attack? Were we about to take fire? We didn't know. We were hyper-vigilant, completely silent, when a Marine commented on a heavy, pungent, odor that engulfed us all. We couldn't identify the smell or locate its source, but eventually realized that it had to come from the land itself. It was the smell of a countryside without infrastructure, without piping, plumbing, or treatment plants. It was the smell of soil gone old and decrepit, ground that had lost its nutrients hundreds of years ago. There were cows in the field in the direction I was facing and they were emaciated, because the grass had dried up into something that even hungry cows would not eat. So they stood there, skinny and scrawny, not moving, as though they were thin, tiny cardboard cut-outs of cows set on a piece of parched plywood in someone's basement on top of which a kid's model train circled. They looked lost too and as out of place as the man I had seen wandering the desert, or the occasional house we passed, stuck in the sand, without a yard, a neighborhood, or a nearby town. As lost and as out of place as we must have looked.

I was behind the wheel and Copas, my assistant driver, was in the front passenger seat. When I was looking to the left for some-

thing suspicious, he was looking off to the right. Anything out of
the ordinary was suspicious. Usually the roadways were bare, so if
we saw a pile of trash alongside the road, it was suspicious. An
abandoned refrigerator or a dead animal alongside the road was
suspicious. A meals-ready-to-eat box was and a soda can was too,
because that was how insurgents would disguise Improvised Explosive Devices. The media reported that they were hidden under piles
of human feces and inside live sheep that would be herded close to
the roads that convoys traveled along. These bombs would be
strapped to pedestrians and hidden in vehicles. We would be driving down the road in a convoy and there would be vehicles trying
to cut in between our trucks. It could have been a bicycle or a
motorcycle, a car or a pickup truck. Copas' responsibility was to
ensure that they stayed away. We had been taught hand gestures
that the Iraqis understood to mean, "Stop!" We learned not to use
the left hand for gestures and, when pointing, to do so not with a
single finger, but with the entire right hand. We were taught to
shout out certain phrases as we drove along, which, to the Iraqis,
meant, "Do not do anything that we might interpret as a threat!"
Words and phrases like "awgaf!" and "le tet-harak!" Our uniforms
helped to intimidate the Iraqis, who easily distinguished our digital
cammies from the standard issue of the Army's infantry. Many
Iraqis believed that to become a Marine, a person had to first take
another's life, through an initiation ritual of sorts. Their level of fear
and eagerness to obey when around us reflected this belief. If for
some reason a vehicle didn't stop, there were Marines in the back of
the Humvee who would point their weapons at them and that
would usually be enough. The A driver picks up what the driver
misses, and the Marines in the back look over us. We worked
together, like fingers on a hand. Seven Marines in a Humvee are not
seven distinct individuals, each in his or her own universe, day-
dreaming or talking to a distant acquaintance on a cell phone or
listening to his own music on an iPod. We are not the same as a
group of seven typical American teenagers driving to the beach.

Instead, we are parts of a single organism, each carrying out a particular set of responsibilities that allow for the vehicle and its occupants to arrive at its destination in one piece. We are a single organism. An invasion force does what it does, not for itself, but so others can get to their bases safely. Marines can sleep in tents at night because there are other Marines awake in foxholes along the camp's periphery. This kind of connectivity requires a deep trust in one another and it generates a deep bond, a closeness of brothers. And, to a great but somewhat lesser degree, brothers and sisters.

I had not slept in days and was exhausted. When I started to get sleepy, I told Copas he had to keep me awake. He talked to me about home and his daughter and the activities they shared, and then about everything else he could think of, just to keep me from falling asleep. Before long, we were joking around and I asked if he knew of any of the travel games that kids play in cars. He did not. "You've got to learn these games, Copas," I said. "Pretty soon your little girl's going to be fidgety in the back of the car on a long drive. You'll have to entertain her. Educate her." I recalled one word game that required one person say a word that begins with the letter "A," then the next a word that begins with the letter "B," and so on. The sequencing of the words has to make sense so that they develop into sentences, then into a story line. Copas and I drove through the desert creating stories about *Giraffes Hitting Ice Junkies* and *A Big Circus Dance.*

Most explosions and most deaths occurred on and around bridges. The insurgents hid on top of them or underneath them and watched as we approached. Our orders were to drive slowly to the bridge and then gun it when passing over or under it. We always saw people on top of and under the bridges and we wondered if one were holding a remote detonator and, if so, which one. *Which one has a grenade? Which one has his crosshairs on us?* There was no way to tell. The Iraqis wore long, shapeless, cotton clothes under which anything could be hidden. The bridges were scary to drive under and scarier to drive over. Insurgents constructed what were called "daisy chains," or a series of interconnected explosives. A single detonator could trigger a number of bombs that could blow up several vehicles in the convoy rather than just one. There may be four or five simultaneous explosions, or there may be a single explosion, then another and another and another. The blasts may hit different vehicles in the convoy, trapping the still unscathed trucks in between the burning ones. The convoy may continue driving through dense clouds thick with smoke and debris, only to fall through the air, truck by truck, where a demolished bridge had stood seconds before.

Driving through villages was a challenge too. We couldn't get too close to the vehicle in front of us because it could explode and we might get trapped. Yet we couldn't fall too far behind it either as that could allow a car or bicycle or pedestrian to get in among the vehicles—although, when you think about it, we were the ones getting in *their* way; it was *their* village, after all. They really should not be that close to us, but they are trying to cross the street, so what was I suppose to do? Children would run into the road and a burdensome decision would fall upon the drivers. We want to stop—any human being would want to stop—but we are in a convoy, with each vehicle moving at the same speed and maintaining a precise distance from the one in front of it, and the child might want to slow us down because his uncle has an automatic weapon and is standing on a roof thirty yards away. It might mean a child's life or a Marine's life. Normally, a driver would say, without a second thought, "It's my life." But it is not just his life. It is the lives of all of the Marines who are in the Humvee, and maybe even the ones who are behind it. Or in front of it. .

Sometimes the locals would be cheering us as we drove through their village. Other times, they would be screaming at us and throwing things at us. Occasionally they would yell something in English, but as the driver, I was so focused on maintaining our place in the convoy and not getting lost, I couldn't make out what they were saying, exactly, but I knew it wasn't a welcoming greeting. I do not recall seeing women alongside the roads, just men and small boys.

At one point we were driving through a village that was completely razed. Houses were half-standing. Doors were broken off hinges. A ghost town. No one. Nothing. We could see the dilapidated houses and the leftovers of the village. Cars abandoned. Stray dogs. It hadn't really hit me that we were in Iraq until I saw that devastation. I was struck less by the remnants of the village in front of me than I was by what *wasn't* there. My eyes searched for them, but I couldn't find intact houses, moving vehicles, living people. My brain tried without success to make sense of what wasn't there.

The men and women who came through during the initial invasion had to do this so that we could pass through this village successfully and get to our camp. They had to do this for us to have a chance of passing through alive. Marines do not talk about what they did during the initial invasion. They may say, "Well, we cleared a village." But a village cannot simply be "cleared," like a kitchen table is cleared for a poker game. The process of "clearing a village" can be logically and verbally explained: it means we go into a house, we get the people out, we tell them to leave the village. That's how it can be explained. The reality of it is that there is a house with a family in it and a bunch of Marines kick open the door and maybe throw in a smoke grenade, maybe not. They have their rifles loaded and ready and are pointing them at the mother or father or kids, and are yelling at them to get out. You know that there were people who did not want to leave. *How could there not have been?* There had to be some who refused to go. *How could there not have been?* The people who refused to go were the corpses we saw as we drove through what had been their village. Killed. Splattered. There was blood on the walls. On the doors. In the streets. On the cars. It wasn't Marine blood. It was civilian blood. There were bodies. *Who was going to pick them up?* There was no way the families would come back: they'd be scared for their lives, and rightfully so. The invading Marines had to keep moving. We could not stop to clean up the mess that was left behind. This is what the invading Marines—boys and girls, who, only recently had been advancing down the field during a high school football game or rushing a freshmen fraternity—had to do for us to pass through safely.

This was just before we got to Taqaddum.

One man walking, alone, in the middle of nothing, like a solitary man on the moon. It didn't make sense. (Photo courtesy of David Leeson)

2

Mortuary Affairs

---

*As the U.S. military death toll mounts in Iraq, the
trauma on the overall force is softened by the fact
that the fallen troops come from different battalions
and different companies. In a force of 30,000
Marines, for example, only a few will be able to say
they knew someone who died.*

*But for the 20 members of the Marine mortuary
affairs unit in this former Iraqi air base west of
Baghdad, each person lost to combat or accident
becomes a personal memory as they gather the body
parts at the scene, sift through possessions and prepare
the often mangled body for shipment back to the
United States.*

From: "Unit Prepares Fallen Troops for the Journey Home,"
by Tony Perry, *Los Angeles Times*, May 23, 2004

A month earlier we were in another desert, at Twentynine Palms in Death Valley, California. It was the first part of February, 2004, and the war in Iraq was worsening. A group of Marines who thought they had missed out on the opportunity to serve in the Middle East were gathered in a metal garage when they heard the good news. There was a need for volunteers for the Corp's first officially declared Mortuary Affairs unit for active duty Marines, to be located in Al Anbar province. The moment the request was made, hands shot up.

Two weeks later, twenty of us met for the first time to start two weeks of training. There was Grinell who was Native American. He was athletic and quiet. We called him Nelly. Gonzalez came from Chicago and, like every Gonzalez in the Marines, he became Gonzo. Moran, a disc jockey from Chicago, became DJ Razor. Why the "Razor" I do not know. We had a reservist named Troescher who we called Trash Can because we couldn't pronounce his name with its weird spelling and string of vowels. Slater was a bald, completely built Louisiana boy, and a total nutritionist. We called him Bucket. Rodriguez—Ro—was from Texas; she was small, had really long hair, and had been a cook before volunteering for Mortuary Affairs. McLaughlin—"M.C"—was a California boy. Cotnoir was from Boston and had the thick accent to prove it. He was the only other reservist among us, but because he was tough enough and was a mortician in civilian life we accepted him, despite the fact that he wasn't active duty. We came up with a variation of the end of Pineda's name and called him Tayta. Also a Californian, he was a hilarious kid, always playing pranks and invariably in a good mood. Sergeant Don Johnson was also from California. He didn't really get a nickname, maybe because he wanted one so much, but only a good one. He wanted a Hispanic nickname because they made you look cooler and more of a badass than the English ones did. He kept asking the platoon what the Spanish word for "boss" was, but no one would tell him. Johnson seemed to be one of those white guys who believed he wasn't a member of a real race, one with a sufficiently rich or substantive culture, and he therefore felt obliged to emulate the ways of those who were so blessed. Eventually, he learned the Spanish word for boss and nailed a three-foot wide sign with "*El Jefe*" painted on it over the doorway to his room. Despite his persistent effort, we would address him only as "Sergeant." Instead of becoming an exotic, ethnic badass, Johnson became a rank, a predetermined slot in an impersonal hierarchy. Our Chief Warrant Officer was James Patterson, who we named *The* Sir, with an emphasis on "*The*" to highlight the fact that he was the most awesome officer around.

Occasionally, a Marine wouldn't like his nickname—Bucket and Trash Can, for example, didn't seem too fond of theirs. But the nicknames stuck, and if one wasn't liked by the owner, it stuck harder. For one thing, they were functional in that they afforded us some small degree of playful control over who we were, and in that way they reminded us that we were still a part of that greater humanity in the real world. They also streamlined our interactions in situations in which efficiency could save a life. It was no longer Rodriguez, but Ro'. Gonzalez was now Gonzo. And neither Grinell nor Goodell any longer had to snap their head toward whatever direction the other's name was called from.

The women were assigned nicknames by the men who reminded them of how they were perceived, what they were seen as, names like Legs and Dolly, names that were unshakable and became what the women were called, at least behind their backs. Gender impacted how we referred to one another in a second way: if several of us were discussing a fellow Marine with whom one of us may not be familiar, we'd refer to him by his last name or by his nickname or by his job or unit. But if that person was a woman, we'd identify her as the "*female*" this or that. He's, "Benson, the mechanic." She's, "Anderson, the *female* mechanic." She's always a female first and a Marine second. That's just the way it was.

If nicknames individualized us to a small degree, they could also remind us that we were all the same. There was a generic nickname that was at various times applied to each and every one of us. *"Hey, 'devil,' where you going?"* we might ask one another. A popular cadence wanted to know, *"What's the sound of a devil dog?"* and the platoon, in unison, would respond by barking twice. *"Woof! Woof!"* we would shout back.

We were from different parts of the country, had different racial, ethnic and religious backgrounds, and varying socio-economic statuses. We also represented a wide range of jobs in the Corps: we were mechanics, motor transportation operators, NBC technicians, communication specialists, military police, supply clerks, and cooks. Just about the only commonality among us was that we were all Marines and we all volunteered to form this Mortuary Affairs unit.

The first thing The Sir had us do was run, and right away I noticed that Ro was keeping up with the rest of us. I saw that as a good sign. Maybe she wasn't going to fall into that typical female Marine role in which she'd slack off, not pull her weight, and expect special favors from the guys. A lot of the women did that and you could tell which ones would just by watching them run. They'd fall out early. I knew this is what happens, because I had seen it a hundred times and so by this point, I would watch for it. But Rodriguez ran long enough and fast enough for me to see that she trained, prepared, and did what a Marine was supposed to do.

There are female Marines in this male Marine Corps who manage to avoid becoming stereotypical "female Marines," and become top-notch Marines. Flat-out superb Marines. Period. They run longer and faster than their male counterparts; they meet their weight and fitness regs better than the males do; they can do more pull-ups; they have higher rifle range scores and have earned a higher belt designation in the martial arts; they do their jobs more responsibly; they are more squared away. Maybe Ro would prove to be one of these Marines.

These women would like to be judged by the accepted standards that define a "good" Marine, even if those standards evolved from an exclusively male culture, whereas many of the men would prefer to judge them first by their gender, to see them as *females* who happen to be Marines. This is especially true of those men who don't run as fast or shoot as straight or aren't as fit. It's not talked about, but there is a more or less constant struggle over this issue. Will these good Marines be judged as Marines first or as females first?

The males remind the females and one another all the time that the females are, well, female. They tell dirty jokes to make the females blush, or refer to the females as "Marine-ettes." The women may emulate the men, even to the point of assuming the loud, curt, male Marine voice, language, and gestures—that, however, typically doesn't work. Frustrated, they occasionally try to challenge the entrenched culture of male superiority. *What will Ro do?* I wondered, as I watched her run.

During this two-week stretch, we were given a series of thick, syrupy anthrax immunizations and, on several afternoons, those among us who were married, were allowed to visit spouses. One day we were sent to Admin to write out wills and power of attorney forms. We were young and many of us hadn't been deployed before, so the meaning of our act was lost on us. We could have been signing another cell phone contract.

Later that afternoon, when we did an inventory of all of the gear we were bringing with us to Iraq, I filled a quadcon—a large, bulletproof storage container—with body bags. Even then I still had little sense of the significance of the sheer number of bags I was packing, or of their impending function.

The training sessions were taught by two officers who showed us how to complete the reams of necessary paperwork. One form had the outline of a body and they showed us how to mark where wounds were and where tattoos were and they explained how we should describe them. We were taught to shade black the Marine's missing body parts on the outline. Another form was for information regarding the identification of the body, such as the Marine's name, social security number, and unit. We Marines would not only process remains, but we would also assume search and recovery responsibilities. We did mock runs to a site where plastic body parts and pieces of raw meat had been scattered around and we were taught how to cordon off the area and how to mark all of the body pieces, and how to pick them up and sort them and organize them. The instructors held up or pointed to pieces of search and recovery equipment. A personal effects bag, a human remains pouch, a litter, a rectangular aluminum transfer case. They demonstrated how to wear the hazardous materials suits, the gloves, and the surgical and respiration masks. They talked about a "remains timeline" that specified the number of days from when a casualty was brought into our bunker or picked up to when they would arrive at Dover Air Force base back in the world. They discussed how to preserve the remains by housing them in large refrigerated trucks—reefers—that were kept running on generators. Throughout, we were shown how to safeguard the remains and how to treat them reverently. At the end of the last training session, our instructors mentioned PTSD—Post Traumatic Stress Disorder. "It's a real thing," they assured us. "Like the flu," they said.

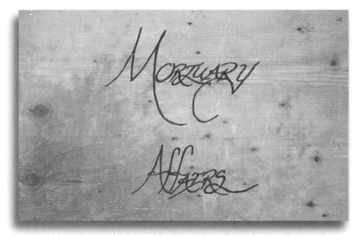

Maddox wrote this sign that we placed in the bunker so that other units would know our location. (Author collection)

3

Camp TQ

---

*Camp Ridgeway / FOB Ridgeway was renamed
Camp Taqaddum when the US Marine Corps cast
off the Army's monikers for their new homes as part
of a wider USMC effort to put an Iraqi face on the
Corps' mission. Camp Taqaddum is located approxi-
mately 74 kilometers west of Baghdad . . .*

*An order issued March 25, 2004, by I MEF's
commanding general, directed that all base names
be changed immediately. As a result, and to connect
with the local communities, the new camps' names
were associated with the local urban or geographical
areas that they are near.*

Camp Taqaddum [aka TQ]
—Globalsecurity.org

The base, roughly 50 miles west of Baghdad, between Fallujah and Ramadi, hadn't been set up yet. It was in the process of being constructed. The initial invasion took over the airport and it became a part of our base. The US had control of the land, but we had to build the base.

When we arrived, everything was disorganized. For example, there were 35 females in a tent designed for eight. Cots were so close together that it was impossible to walk between them. There was no place to put the gear, so it was placed at the heads of the cots, next to the tent walls, pushing them outward. That tent was a microcosm of the base. After a week or so, we started to get organized. "Mortuary Affairs over this way, Heavy Equipment mechanics over here. Motor Transport over there!"

We lived in tents that had plywood floors. The tents' canvas had been dipped in kerosene to repel the mosquitoes—even though that would mean that if one were hit by mortar fire, it—and then the others—would go up in a flash. Right? It doesn't make sense to soak canvas in kerosene and then spread it out in a war zone, but that's what we were told. Although there was air conditioning hooked up to generators, both were constantly breaking down due to the stress of running continuously and the sand blowing into them. It was not uncommon for the power to shut down and, with it, our tent's two light bulbs that were used to illuminate the books from home that we read at night, and the refrigerator, which held our cold water. The tents were surrounded by reinforcing sand bags.

Mortuary Affairs had two tents that were designated for the males and were separated from the others in Tent City. They were about a mile from the bunker, in a back area, outside of Tent City proper, away from where the other Marines lived. The females slept together regardless of their MOS or job, so the two MA females had no choice but to sleep in the same tent with women from other units. The Sir slept in the MA bunker.

The airfield was on a plateau, which was strategically smart.

Razor and concertina wire circled the base. There were guard houses or posts along the periphery of the camp. Each guard post was staffed with two Marines who kept watch. Also along the perimeter were holes in the ground from where the grunts kept watch so the rest of us could sleep at night and function during the day.

The camp was so big it was divided into sections. There was an initial area, a processing center, where Marines were sent when they first came in to get set up and reorganized and regrouped. Tent City was the main part of the base, where the majority of people lived, at least initially. There was another large area on base set up for mechanics to work on the gear that broke down. Where else could we keep the gear that was down? We didn't want to keep it where anyone who wanted to could see it. Perhaps it was because we had civilians on base. We did not want the locals to see what gear we had or which pieces of it were down, so most of our equipment was kept in a separate area of the base.

The locals were contracted by the U.S. to help us. They took care of us. They assisted us when we set up the Internet, for example. They did our laundry. They got rid of our trash and helped set up the tents and the trailers. They helped set up the water systems. There were Turks who came in to help set up the port-a-johns and to perform maintenance. Also, there was a local restaurant that, like the airport, had been there prior to our arrival and had stayed. The U.S. asked those Iraqis to cook food for the Marines. They lived and worked there and prepared loads of Iraqi food for us, such as shawarma, which were slabs of lamb on vertical skewers that would rotate while cooking. The Iraqi cooks would slice off the outside of the meat and serve it with bread they baked in a stone oven.

Other locals would sell DVDs and trinkets from tiny stores and still others comprised working details, groups of manual laborers who we'd have to watch while they worked. We were instructed to keep our weapons loaded and on fire and aimed at them the entire time that they were working. Then we'd have lunch with them. It was a strange feeling aiming a loaded weapon at other human beings engaged in an activity as innocent and mundane as eating lunch. When we had our lunch, they would offer us their food, though they were the ones without much food, whose entire lives were in turmoil. They would say, in broken English, "You've been working so long, you've been working so hard, when are *you* going to eat?" And we would say, "We eat later." They offered us whatever they were eating and shared it with us as we pointed our weapons at them. The other Iraqis who were on base were nice too, like the men who worked at the restaurant. In my off time, I would play soccer with them.

Mortuary Affairs had our own bunker in an old Iraqi Air Force hangar, which was one of the safest locations on base. The roof of the bunker was part of the ground, rising up from the sand. We could get up onto the bunker's roof by going out and walking along the ground, which rose gradually and became the roof. We arranged green sandbags on the sloping roof to spell out what we believed and what we lived: "No One Left Behind," and "Honor, Respect, Reverence." From the back, sides and top the bunker resembled a sand hill or berm. From straight on, it was a building, with a wall and doors. When the sun was behind the facility a narrow shadow was cast along the façade. That sliver of shade lowered the desert temperature by only a few degrees, but that was sufficient to draw us to it. Eventually, we built and set up picnic tables covered with camouflage netting along the shaded margin of sand. We would sit and talk and, as our deployment wound down, smoke cigars and think of home.

When we first entered the bunker, it was completely empty inside. We had to set up everything from scratch. We designed and built the rooms we needed, made the tables we'd use for processing, ran electrical wires, and hooked up the lights and phone. Having received generators we connected them to the air conditioning so the place would be cooler, adjusting the refrigerators and the coolers to be as cold as they had to be. We needed a room in which

Marines could stand post. We needed a room for The Sir. A conference room was required in order to interview survivors. There were three bedrooms with cots in them: one for Sergeant Johnson, another for Sergeant Cotnoir, and a third, containing a bunk bed, for random, exhausted Marines to sleep in when processing was particularly long. The bodies started coming in. And we kept getting bodies and we kept getting bodies, so we never really finished the construction work.

This is where we worked inside the bunker. The bunker was empty when we arrived. It was our platoon that built the walls, rooms, and work stations. Marines in our platoon ran the wires and hooked up the electricity along the perimeter of the bunker. On the work tables can be seen biohazard bags, goggles, scissors, and gauze. Black body bags are on litters with saw dust to absord any liquids and sand bags to support the litters. (Author collection)

4

Processing

In Operation Enduring/Iraqi freedom, USMC Mortuary Affairs (MA) personnel were tasked with the "processing" of dead bodies. The processing involved the collection of remains, collecting and cataloguing personal effects, making the bodies as presentable as possible, and in the case of U.S. personnel, getting them ready for transport to Dover Air Force Base where further processing takes place. The dead included U.S. military personnel, civilians (including an embedded American journalist), and enemy military personnel.

OIF MORTUARY AFFAIRS DE-BRIEFINGS: "HELPING THOSE WHO HANDLE THE DEAD," Captain Joseph Pecorelli, MSC, USNR, Captain Mark Long, MSC, USNR, Captain James Young, MC, USNR, Commander (SEL) Victor Sheldon, CHC, USNR, and Captain Richard Frederick, MSC, USNR
—*Department of Navy online document, 2004*

They brought in the first body. The grunts brought him in. There weren't lights in the middle of the bunker yet, only along the side of the wall, so we put the body there and then we . . . did nothing. Although we had been trained, we didn't know what to do next. We were taught, but we didn't know. They took the time to tell us what to expect, but when the first body came in, several of us froze. We became inept and couldn't do anything, really. We just didn't know . . . we just couldn't. . . . We knew how to complete the paper work and what to had to be done, but when it's real, when it's no longer an abstract thought and when it's in your face, in front of you, you stand there, motionless, wondering, *What do I do?*

The Sir had called in every person in our platoon and designated people to particular tasks. He said, "You two are going to carry, you two are going to turn the body over, and you two are going to do the paper work." He wanted all of us there, I'm certain, so that we could help each other out, help each other deal with it, because I'm sure that the Sir thought that we might panic and maybe we weren't going to be able to do this. After all, most of us were eighteen and twenty year old kids still. If we didn't know it, The Sir did.

He gave us step-by-step instructions. "Roll him over to document his wounds." We may have known that a Marine was hit by bullets or a grenade, but we may not have known where. But when we tried to turn him over, we couldn't. Rigor mortis was setting in and he was already beginning to stiffen, except for his waist, which was like a pivot point. Even when we strained to turn him over, we could not. It was awkward and we were silent except for The Sir's slow, calm, firm instructions. "C'mon guys, you were trained on this and you know what to do," he reassured us. And so, eventually, we did it. "Okay," The Sir said, "now write down any distinguishing marks, any tattoos." So we did. "Now, write down which body parts are missing and shade the missing parts black on the outline of the body." So we did. We followed The Sir's directions, marking the wounds, drawing the tattoos, shading the missing parts black. We had to be told throughout what to do next and how to do it.

After the first body, the processing went smoother. The Sir organized us into teams of four, which were usually then divided into two members who would be the "hands on" for the body and two who would complete the paper work. In time, a process of sorts evolved. A body would come in and we'd remove every item from the pockets and inventory all of the gear that was on him. We couldn't assume that all of his gear was on him. They don't always have two boots. They don't always have Kevlar helmets or a flak jacket or the things that might be expected to be there. They are gone. Missing. The body parts they covered may be missing too. We then conducted an inventory of all the items that were in the pockets. Exactly what they had on them when they died can then be verified. When down the road the family asks, "Where is this picture? We know he always carried this picture with him," we could report that he did or he did not have it on him when he died. Or if money wasn't there that someone thought was, we could check our inventory. If there had been a pen in their pocket, or a note, if there were two twenties and two ones, we documented it. We would precisely document what he did and did not have on him at the time of his death.

We would inventory everything. Every body had a copy of *The Rules of Engagement* in their left breast pocket. Some would have knives or earplugs, food, a spoon. Pens. Rolled up pieces of paper, a scribbled reminder to ask their mother to send Skin So Soft or Blue Star Ointment to keep the sand fleas away, a scrunched up wrapper, trash that wasn't thrown away—trash that would now become part of a family's lasting memories of a son, husband, brother, father, hero.

There were pictures. A man and his wife and daughter. A farmhouse and barn in Iowa. Many were the pictures teenagers would carry back home. A high school student with his football teammates. A young man in a sleeveless t-shirt leaning against a 1983

Camaro. A letter in which a Marine tells his widow that he is now dead, but that he loves her still, and he wants her to give their daughter a kiss from him.

Some items were uncommon, like the sonogram of a fetus. Some were not uncommon enough, like a suicide note.

We would examine the remains for distinguishing traits such as birthmarks, scars and tattoos. Where are they on the body? What is their approximate size? How can they be described? We would write down the wounds that were on the body. If there are bullet wounds, where on the body are they? If they are in the head, where in the head? How many? We would get the appropriate form and mark the outline of the body with dots or Xs where the Marine was hit. Where body parts were missing, we would shade those parts of the outline black. If a part of the head was missing, we'd shade that area black.

We tried to identify each body, but that wasn't always easy. They may have their dog tags on, they may not. It was not unusual for a body to have missed-matched dog tags. It could be that a kid was wearing someone else's dog tags, even though it was against regulations. Maybe they have their military ID in their wallet, but maybe they don't. Their name might be on their blouse or trousers or cover, but it might not be readable, if it is there at all. When you share a tent or small hole with others, belongings get mixed up. Items such as these do not always match up, which is why we would write down everything a person had on them. Initially, we finger-printed them but did not continue the practice for very long because it became too difficult. There were not always fingers. Or the fingers were stuck in the position they were in when the Marine died, as if still holding his M-16, for example, and we could not unbend them easily.

We would then put the remains into a clean body bag and put the bag into a metal box we called an aluminum transfer case, similar to a coffin. We then placed the case in a reefer where it stayed cool. When it was time to take it to the flight deck to go home, we would drape an American flag over it and carry out a processional, a separate one for each set of remains. Four of us, one at each corner of the case, would walk it through two rows of Air Force personnel who were there to do the flying. They would all salute the remains as we walked them through. They would salute as if they were saluting the President of the United States, as if they were saluting their own fallen family members. Ramrod straight backs, their arms at a 45-degree angle. There was such a strong emotion contained in that salute, such a fierce intensity embedded in the ritual, that it never subsided, even after too many processionals. In fact, it got stronger. Each time we came away from it knowing in our hearts that we were all Marines, and that we were in this together. Each time we'd walk back to the bunker ready once more to go on.

If each processional strengthened our resolve, it also removed us a bit further from the mainstream of the Camp. As the causalities increased, so did the possibility of death and the awareness of what it was that the men and women of Mortuary Affairs did. Our platoon was to the Marines what the Marines are to much of America: we did things that had to be done but that no one wanted to know about.

The processionals and the nature of our work in general also impacted us as individuals. Before the Corps and the war and Mortuary Affairs, death seemed to occur rarely and to people who were old; another's body was off limits, often sacred, not to be touched without permission, and certainly not to be pieced together like a sad, gruesome puzzle; social isolation was temporary and voluntary, and ostracism was unheard of except when someone had done something unspeakably wrong. All of these taken for granted understandings changed for us.

The army set up a perimeter and stood post while we tried our best to change our socks, use the head, brush our teeth, and find a place to sleep.
(Photo courtesy of Bill Thompson)

5

Pressure

---

*Up to one in five of the American military personnel
in Iraq will suffer from post-traumatic stress disorder,
say senior forces' medical staff dealing with the
psychiatric fallout of the war . . . At least 22 US
soldiers have killed themselves—a rate considered
abnormally high—mostly since President George
Bush declared an end to major combat on 1 May
last year. These suicides have led to a high-level
Department of Defense investigation, details of
which will be disclosed in the next few weeks.*

From: "Stress Epidemic Strikes American Forces in Iraq,"
Peter Beaumont, *The Guardian* (UK),
January 25, 2004

Every Marine has the responsibility to maintain the Corp's body composition regulations. Two times a year, at least, Marines are weighed and if our weight exceeds the maximum allowable, our body fat is measured. If we do not meet regs, we're enrolled in a body composition program. Marines also have to be physically fit, combat ready. This is essential to self-discipline and character. If Marines are not physically fit, we are a detriment to our unit. Our fitness is measured by our performance during a series of events, involving pull-ups, abdominal crunches, and a three mile run. Official measurements and sanctions are in place to keep Marines within regs—including, theoretically, discharge from the Corps. Informal sanctions exist as well.

An overweight Marine really isn't fat, and an out-of-shape one isn't actually unfit; if they were in the outside world, if they were civilians walking down Main Street, no one would find them disgusting. Here, they are and it is not acceptable. They are not acceptable as Marines. In the Corps and on base they are called "fat nasties" and "shit bags" and they are told they must change.

At one time we had a Marine with us who was overweight. He was an E3. The higher ranked E4s said to him, "You need to be squared away, marine. And do you know who is going to square you away? The platoon is going to square you away." The E4s approached those of us who were lower ranking but who held billets or certain authority responsibilities, and told us we needed to square that Marine away. He became a virtual slave to whomever he was assigned and, as such, he was made to do all of the nasty things, all of the dirty things, all of the most disgusting things. If he mouthed off or talked back, we had him do push-ups. When one of us wore him out, we handed him off to another.

The corporals put us in charge of this Marine and we did what was expected of us. We made him dig a hole—a fire hole or fox hole—with his e-tool that was exactly one rifle wide and two rifles long, dimensions specific enough to imply the hole had some specific purpose. Then we would have him fill it up again. Nonsense.

Terrible, miserable nonsense. Because this Marine couldn't run fast enough, he was assigned to the runners of the platoon, to those of us who could run well. We were in charge of running him and wearing him out. And so we ran him until he puked. If he didn't puke, we hadn't done our job, we hadn't run him long enough, we hadn't run him fast enough, or the run wasn't vigorous enough. It was like hazing. Heck, it was hazing. We calculated the length of a football field and made him bear crawl to the end and back. We had him do monkey fuckers all the way down the field and star jumps all the way back. All very demanding exercises. The bear crawl necessitated walking on all fours, with the knees off the ground. The monkey fuckers required bending down and grabbing your ankles, then crouching down like a baseball catcher, standing back up, then dropping back down. Star jumps involved squatting down, then jumping high into the air, and throwing out your hands and feet so that your body forms the rough outline of a star. By the end of each session, when this Marine was beat, completely whipped, he'd be told that he had five minutes to shower and get back to the field, which was impossible to do.

When he returned, not showered and foul-smelling, every other Marine would be screaming in his face that he's a fucking fat nasty and he fucking smells and is fucking disgusting and that he is a shit-bag Marine. This treatment continues and does not stop until every single Marine in the platoon is on his back and down his neck.

If anything would square away a shit bag, this would. You would think. But it didn't. In fact, I've never seen it work. I've only seen it make a Marine fake it, fake like he gives a fuck. I've also seen it not work, like it didn't for this one Marine whose remains we processed.

On this occasion we were called out on a convoy to another base to pick up a Marine who had killed himself. This Marine went into a port-a-john with his rifle, pushed it up under his chin, and blew his head onto the walls. Slater, Cotnoir, and Maddox went to

get him. They removed the body from the port-a-john, then re-
trieved the rest of the remains. They had to peel and pull off chunks
of flesh and brain tissue that had sprayed the walls. They brought
all of it back to the bunker and I started the paperwork. The Sir
told me to interview the Marines in his unit to find out what they
knew and why, in their opinion, the victim took his own life.

Marines wear a green t-shirt over which is a digi-blouse which
contains a rank insignia. The Sir said, "Goodell, take off your
blouse and talk to these Marines and find out what you can." He
wanted to eliminate possible hierarchy concerns by concealing my
rank. This relieved both parties of formal deference issues and
allowed acceptance of the reality of the situation and the feelings
that accompanied it. The Marines had found a suicide note. When
I asked for it to put with his personal effects, they offered only a
copy rather than the original. As they were searching for the original, I sat down and read the copy. The deceased wrote that he could
not live up to expectations, that his platoon sergeant and squad
leaders were constantly yelling at him and trying to square him
away. He wasn't a good enough Marine. His squad leaders were
relentless in conveying their disgust, telling him that he was falling
out of runs, and that he needed to square himself away because he
was a shit-bag Marine. He agreed that he wasn't good enough, not
for the Corps. He wrote that he could take no more.

As I read the note, which focused on him not being a good
enough Marine, I was struck by the fact that it was written on camouflage paper, which made me think that he obviously had the
Marine Corps in his heart. This is the stationery purchased by
young Marines, new Marines, who are all *hoorah!* and proud to be
in the Corps. They buy camouflage designed and colored writing
paper and envelopes to write home to their parents and friends,
their girlfriends or boyfriends, their high school teachers.
Regardless of what the proud Marine actually writes, the stationery
itself says to them all, "You didn't think I'd make anything of
myself, did you? But look at me now!" The paper itself had me

thinking that he still was motivated, even if he wasn't a good enough Marine. He obviously identified with the Corps and wanted others to think of him as a Marine. He had the Corps in his heart, still. Why, then, would he take his life and cite the Corps and its expectations as the cause? The whole matter seemed discrepant, so rather than put the copy with the rest of the paperwork, I decided to wait until I could examine the original note. When I finally did, the contradiction was resolved. The original note was in fact written on plain white paper. The camouflage effect on the copied note was made by his own blood and guts that had seeped through his clothing and onto the paper in his pocket.

I don't know why the Marines take kids like this one who are overweight by Marine standards, kids who aren't natural runners. They must know that this is going to happen to them. It is inevitable. Marines are trained to kill, to become warriors. We're taught to be hard core. We're taught that pain is only weakness leaving the body. This makes it hard for some recruits to make the cut and it makes it easy for us to forget that that kid, the one who can't make the cut, who can't run fast enough or run long enough, the one who is not in the best shape, has a mother at home who loves him and who prays everyday for his safe return. Instead, we see him as tarnishing the image of the Corps, as being the weakest link in the chain, as being the guy who could get the whole unit killed. Sad. Tough. Real tough. And when these Marines commit suicide, we are trained to think of them as cowards. In bootcamp, Marine Combat Training (MCT), and at our duty stations, we're told that suicide is for cowards and it's the weak way out. A First Sergeant walks in—he's a high ranking man—to lecture us about suicide, and he tells us that the Corp is better off without those cowards. Nobody says, "Man, we shouldn't treat these Marines like this. Maybe we need to reorganize our structure or the way we do things. Maybe we need to offer leadership classes that will teach officers how to get these Marines within weight and regs, instead of allowing them to fall victim to suicide."

What makes it even harder to understand is that the female Marines aren't subject to the same treatment. Female Marines who don't make regs aren't called shit bags or fat nasties. They're called "*typical* female Marines." They're called "bags of nasties." It's as though the Corps, deep in its soul, believes that males who don't meet regs fail because they choose to fail, but the females who don't meet regs fail for a reason beyond their control. They fail because they are female. Females aren't held back by a single shortcoming that can be remedied, like being fat or lazy. They're held back by what they are, and that cannot be overcome. They are the embodiment of flaws. They are bags of nasties.

Mortuary Affairs is about to go on a convoy. Our vehicles are lined up with two Humvees in the front and Maddox in the turret of the seven ton with the 50 cal. Our only protection in the Humvees was the sandbags we used to line the floor in the back. There were no extra protective plates or lining on these vehicles. (Author collection)

6

Convoys

FORWARD OPERATING BASE RIDGEWAY—
*As Marines continue rolling into Iraq, leaders in
Kuwait bustle to outfit as many military convoys
as possible with extra protection for passengers from
ambushes and improvised explosives commonly used
by insurgents.*

*According to guidance from the I Marine
Expeditionary Force's commanding general, every
effort is to be made to armor the thousands of "soft-
skinned" military vehicles the Marines are bringing
with them to Iraq.*

*Given the tactics currently used by the enemy,
the Marine Corps is eager to add higher levels of
protection to their vehicles, beyond simply requiring
passengers to wear Kevlar helmets and flak jackets
with bulletproof inserts and lining the truck's inside
with sandbags.*

*Protection for most vehicles comes in the form
of add-on kits, which fasten to the chassis or frame.
Metal doors replace canvas; Kevlar blankets or steel
plates cover floorboards and seats; some even have
bulletproof windshields.*

*Yet certain kits are on backorder, meaning some
vehicles may be driven to their forward operating
bases in Iraq with little or no additional protection.*

The area west of Baghdad that the Marines are
moving into contains the hot-spot city of Fallujah,
which has been the site of numerous convoy
ambushes by extremists using rocket-propelled
grenades, assault rifles and improvised explosives.

    Some Marines, worried that the kits wouldn't
reach them in time or even wanting to further
harden the vehicles, have sought out numerous
alternatives.

    Staff Sgt. Charles J. Willson, who oversaw the
staging of I MEF vehicles in Kuwait, was among the
handful of Marines at Camp Victory who scooped up
Humvee armor plating shed by Army units returning
from Iraq.

    "We're doing the Marine thing," said Willson.
"If they're willing to give it to us, we're willing to
take it. We're going to bring all our Marines home."

From: "Marines Hustle to Toughen Iraq-Bound Vehicles,"
by Staff Sergeant Bill Lisbon, *Marine Corps News*, March 15, 2004

It begins with a phone call, with a voice that says, "We have a Marine down!" Or sometimes the voice says that there's a fire fight and there *may* be a Marine down. Or maybe there was an explosion and we don't yet know if anybody has been hurt, so stand by. Sometimes it was for sure and sometimes it was a standby, but it always began with a phone call. We would all come into the shop and prepare for a convoy, not knowing whether we would go or not. The vehicles would be ready, typically three Humvees and a seven ton, which is a large truck with a bed on the back. There was a reefer on the seven ton because we never knew what we'd find. We may be out there for three or four days. We didn't want bodies rotting, so we'd put them in the cold reefer for the trip back to base.

    There were mounts for the machine guns in the back of the Humvees. The 50 Cal machine gun went on top of the seven ton.

The 50 Cal is heavy enough to sometimes require that two Marines work together to mount it. Every Marine had an M-16 and some of them used SAWS (Squad Automatic Weapons). The NCOs (non-commissioned officers) would often give the drivers their 9mms because it was too difficult to pull up and aim your rifle while driving. Every Marine knew where to go, which truck they'd be in, and where in the truck they'd be. The same Marines drove the same vehicles, the same Marines were the gunners, the same Marines loaded the ammo—making sure it matched the weapons and the vehicles they were in—the same people loaded up the weapons. The entire process was ritualized, all of us working together, in the same manner, every time.

On those occasions when a female would drive one of the vehicles, the male Marines weren't happy, and they'd let her know it. "I don't want to ride with *her,*" they'd whine. "She drives too fucking slow!" This despite the fact that on this day she may be the only licensed Humvee driver among them and the convoys were driven at a predetermined distance from the vehicle in front. But that's how the males chose to see it.

Sometimes a female pushed back on that pervasive, amorphous subculture as best she could, trying hard to be seen as a Marine rather than a girl or a *"Marine-ette."* For example, when these tough, built-up, macho guys named their vehicles *"the Green Destroyer"* and *"El Loco del Demonio,"* one female named her Humvee *"Noodle."* The males became irate.

"We're heading out," one told Razor one day. "Load up the *Noodle!*"

"What the fuck you talking like that for?" a male replied. "I'm not going nowhere in no fuckin' Noodle. Fuck that shit!"

When the guys gave similar scary sounding names to their weapons, such as *Killer,* and *Death Rod,* and *Die Hard,* she named hers *Pork Chop.*

Our Alice packs were already in the vehicles in case we had to stay out for a while. There was an extra green t-shirt or two in the pack, perhaps a couple of pairs of underwear and socks, and certainly a container of baby wipes. The drivers started carrying lists of the names, social security numbers, and blood types of all the Marines riding with them, in case something should happen to one of them. Often, we would arrange the vehicles in a certain order, usually the three Humvees followed by the seven ton. Occasionally, that order would change because we needed extra security when traveling long distances. We may have two MP (military police) vehicles, one in front of us and the other in back, helping to provide security. On other occasions, like the day we went to the lake, we had a Navy vehicle in our convoy.

When processing, it was typical for half of the Marines on duty to go on the convoy while the other half stayed back. Those Marines who didn't go, waited, awake, worried, until the others got back. *Were they under attack? Will they get back alive?* They may be back today or tonight, or maybe tomorrow, or maybe not until the next day. It was the job of those who stayed behind to process the remains, but the group that had gone on the convoy often returned with their adrenalin pumping and could neither eat nor sleep, so they often helped process. They had just had their hands in human remains, were knee-deep in it, and therefore did not want to eat. They were still amped up from being on the convoy and could not sleep. There was nothing left for them to do, really, but to see the job through to the end. Then again, no one slept much. Ever. Undeniably, the Marines who went on the convoy had it worse than those who stayed back, but neither group could eat or sleep.

We received a call one day and were told that an IED exploded under an Army convoy that was crossing a bridge, blowing a truck over the side, and down into a ravine. The soldiers in the vehicle that followed reported that it appeared as though the truck had just suddenly disappeared into thin air. What actually happened was that the explosion was powerful enough to send the truck so high into the air that it left the field of vision of the guys behind it. They had thought it simply disappeared. Poof! Until it fell back through their windshield framed vista and rolled down into the ravine below. Everyone was called in, we gathered our weapons and packs and ammo. We brought water and food because we didn't know how long we'd be gone. We climbed into our vehicles and headed out.

When we'd get to the site of an explosion, we never knew if there were other IEDs around. This would happen sometimes. The insurgents would detonate the initial IED and when aid arrived, they would trigger additional ones. As a result, on this convoy we were joined by an Explosives Ordnance Disposal (EOD) team. These Marines see hidden explosives in a way we cannot. EOD personnel are like the Eskimos who recognize different types of snow. Is the snow heavy or light? Wet or dry? Are the flakes falling fast or just moderately fast? Is it fluffy or hard-packed? They can see all of this and much more. When a child sees snow for the first time, all he or she sees is "snow." It may be a pristine snow-covered alp or a black mound by a curbside. It all looks the same. EOD Marines can spot a handful of out-of-place sand from forty yards away and know that it's not right. They may have dogs with them or robots with them, but they didn't on this day. They swept the area, poking at the sand with their knives, squinting and focusing on anything that triggered their attention, which, to me, seemed to be everything.

As they were doing their job securing the area, we walked, in our white plastic suits, gloves and face masks, toward a five foot wide crater in the ground. I looked down and saw a boot. Then I noticed that in the boot was a foot. The seven ton was nearby on its side. We started flagging remains before picking them up. We stuck a red flag attached to a thin wire in the ground here, and there, and there. We reached the seven ton and saw that the body wasn't intact. Only the top half was there. When the vehicle exploded, *everything* inside it exploded. While another unit was on their way to retrieve the vehicle remains, our job was to retrieve the human remains. All of them. There were pieces of burned metal,

burned gear, burned clothing, and burned . . . *everything*. We tried
to figure out what were human remains and what were vehicle
remains. We didn't want to have to tell a mother that her son was
gone and all we had to give her was his head . . . or a limb. We
wanted to send every piece home. So we got everything, every single piece that was covering the vehicle's interior. One reason for our
thoroughness was what had happened to the four American contractors who were apprehended by insurgents in Fallujah. They
were shot, burned, dismembered, and dragged through the streets
behind trucks to cheering crowds. Finally, what remained of them
was hung from a bridge. That was not going to happen again.

Pineda and I pulled the burnt upper torso from the truck and
then removed a leg. Pineda climbed into the cab to collect the rest.
He picked up or peeled off every single one of several pieces covering the vehicle's interior. He could not have been more focused or
dedicated to what he was doing had it been his own mother's
remains, not even if God had told him, "Tayta, collect every single
last piece of your mother's physical body and I'll bring her back to
life." Some of the remains had to be scooped up by putting our
hands together as though we were cupping water. We put the body
parts and pieces from the seven ton and the surrounding ground
into a body bag, then scooped up the liquidy remains and poured
them in too. When we finished, the contents—the clumps and
chunks and pieces and parts—didn't resemble a human body. Nor
did they remain equally distributed within the body bag. If we
picked up the body bag at one end, everything moved to the other
end. When we lifted it at both ends, it all slid to the middle. It
occurred to us to put the body bag on a litter to carry it up the deep
sand of the steep ravine. We placed the remains in the reefer to
protect it from both the heat and the insurgents on the drive to the
base.

Back at the bunker I interviewed the survivors. I learned that
there had been two Army soldiers in the truck, the driver and the
A driver. The driver was able to extricate himself from the wreckage

and was okay, but the A driver was pinned inside and couldn't get out. The overturned vehicle was leaking fuel and a fire had started. The driver had fought with his platoon who were holding him back, pulling him away from the seven ton. "The A driver's still in there," he screamed, "let me go. I know I can get him out." But they would not let go. "The A driver's stuck and we can't get him out," they said. "There's no helping him." While they were arguing with the driver, the vehicle exploded and killed the A driver.

We Marines couldn't understand that. We know that "No Marine left behind" is a slogan, but we also know it's more than that.

The Humvee became the insurgents' favorite target.
(Photo courtesy of Bill Thompson)

7

Stigma

But even combat-toughened Marines prefer not to think about what Mortuary Marines do.

From: "Unit Prepares Fallen Troops for Journey Home," by Tony Perry, *Los Angeles Times*, May 23, 2004

Among the Maori, a group of people living on the islands off the
coast of New Zealand, anyone who in any way handled a corpse
was precluded from interacting with the rest of society. It was
believed that he would contaminate whomever he came into contact with. He was considered too unclean to even touch the food he
ate, so it would often be placed on the ground before him and he
would kneel, bent at the waist, and, with his hands behind his back,
lower his head to the food, and try his best to eat. It doesn't sound
fair, but this reaction is understandable, even though the corpses he
handled were likely still intact, free of the messiness that an explosion brings. Caring for the dead scares not only the caretakers, but
those who come into contact with the caretakers too.

The other Marines seemed to avoid us and because the nature
of our work made it easy to identify us as Mortuary Affairs, we were
easy to avoid. Many of the Marines who came into the bunker had
died from an explosion, and their bodies were burned. The odor
seemed familiar at first but was difficult to identify. One day two
Marines brought chow back to the bunker for the rest of us and
that was it. The bodies smelled like burned meat, which is what
they were. Often dismembered, much of them, sometimes in pieces
and chunks, they smelled like meat left too long on a grill. It
became common for us to throw up. After working many hours
straight, a Marine would bring chow back to the bunker for us and
we would try to eat but would throw up instead. It didn't take long
for food to stop smelling like food and to start smelling like death.
It was no wonder that the Mortuary Affairs Marines lost weight.
When it seemed as though remains were coming in continuously
over a period of time, we would drop weight. When there was a lull,
we regained a few pounds. Our weight seemed to reflect the number of casualties as clearly as a scoreboard.

We were different from the other Marines in additional ways.
The smell of death permeated our clothes, hair, skin, and fingers,
and the remains permanently stained our uniforms. Our cammies
smelled different. They were stained differently, in different pat-

terns in different places and shades. Because we sat alone, together, in the chow hall, forcing down food, the other Marines could easily spot us there too. They stayed away. They didn't want to be around us and we didn't want to be around them. Some thought we'd bring them bad luck, and we didn't want them thinking that. We especially did not want them to know what we knew.

The Marines who shared my tent weren't mean to me, but they weren't my friends either. There was simply nothing there, nothing at all between us. They didn't ask me to go to chow with them. When they went to the PX, they didn't invite me along. When they went to the head or to the chapel, they would ask others to go with them, but never me.

There was one Marine in my tent, Corporal Dennis, who did try to befriend me and, initially, we did do things together. We went to chow, ran, practiced martial arts. I was offered friendship, but, more for Dennis' sake than my own, I refused to accept it. Still, the Corporal kept trying. At one point, I was gone from the tent for three straight days processing remains. On that third night I walked back to the tent alone, covered with death's odor and haunted by its gruesome images. I stumbled to my cot and braced myself to fall onto it when I saw a note on the sleeping bag. It was from Dennis, who, despite my many rebuffs, was still trying to develop a friendship with me. The note asked if we could talk. The previous three days had been trying ones for the Marines of Mortuary Affairs, and here was someone obviously willing to listen . . . wanting to listen, offering me the opportunity to talk. But I did not want to talk. I didn't want to hear myself describing what I had just gone through. I didn't want to fuel the images still fresh in my mind. Nor did I want Dennis to hear about it, to see it, or to even begin to know what I knew. I hit the rack.

Because there were only two females in Mortuary Affairs, they lived in Tent City with the general population. They had to deal not only with the stigma of being in Mortuary Affairs, but with the many challenges of being a female too.

For example, when a female Marine has chow with a male Marine, there's a good chance his objective is not company or a meal, but sex. The assumption made by all who see them at lunch will be that they are involved sexually, and that's what these observers will tell their friends. If she watches a DVD in a male Marine's tent, the same sexual motive is likely present, and the same gossip will follow, even if she is only one of five people gathered around the laptop's screen. If she agrees to PT (physical training) with a male Marine after he swore that he had no ulterior motive, he'll try to persuade her to do a series of squats or another exercise that simulates a sexual position. Of the hundred or so possible exercises they could do, he wants her to drop down as she bends her knees, as her legs open and her shorts loosen and fall away from her thighs. Onlookers will interpret that as a sure sign that they are sleeping with each other. In no time at all, she'll be labeled a slut and placed into the same category as her tent mate who agreed to sleep with every male member of the platoon, in the order in which their beds were arranged in their tent, and who went ahead and did just that. The male Marines who want to sleep with her, but are not, are insulted and perhaps furious. After all, there is no policy prohibiting it and she's already sleeping with everyone else, they believe, so why not with them?

It's unlikely that a female Marine will find much solace or safety or strength among the other females, as so many of them have given into the pressure and have accepted the label. If this young woman doesn't join in on the game, the female Marines will, like their male counterparts, label her too. They'll stigmatize her as a "bitch" or "dyke" or a "prude" or a "religious nut," and they'll find additional evidence of her deviance in her unwillingness to color her hair, to do her nails, or even to apply make-up at 4:30 a.m.—while holding a flashlight in the darkness of the tent.

If working in Mortuary Affairs can be relatively lonely for a female, life in the Marines can be extremely lonely. A woman might be the only female in her platoon, and that fact alone makes her popular, because all the male Marines want to hang out with her. They want to know where she's going for lunch and what she's doing after work. And she wants to give in even though doing so leads to problems. Every day she wants to give in. Every day she wants desperately to go to lunch with them. She wants to party with them. She wants to drink with them. They are her platoon, her Marines, and they are all going out together. A deep loneliness flows through her and not giving into it is hard. It is a terrible pain, an awful existence.

I knew several female Marines who tried to navigate their way through this tangle of derogatory labels and differential treatment by faking having a boyfriend. One carried around a picture of a former boyfriend and talked about him as though he was still in her life. Another found an actual boyfriend, more or less, a Marine, one who was fairly close by, was big, tough, and Hispanic, and was in a leadership position. "Let the male Marines screw around with me now!" she would say. "Let the female Marines talk badly about me now!" she would add. "In either English or Spanish!"

Meanwhile, the male members of the unit had their own tent, one that was not in Tent City, which meant it was farther from the bunker. They were secluded from the general population. They too kept to themselves, and for the same reason. It was easier, especially for the other Marines, for the Mortuary Affairs people to remain apart and it was better for us to stay together. Apart and together. Apart, we didn't have to talk to the other Marines about what we were doing. Among ourselves, there was no need to talk because we already knew. While we were all Marines, our experiences with death differed: most of the others might not have spent a single minute with a single Marine from our camp who died in Iraq.

We were to a degree more like the Marines we processed than we were like those who were still alive. The bodies wore our uniforms and haircuts, were our age, more or less, and did not fear or avoid us. And unlike the men and women who were still breathing and fighting, these Marines now understood clearly and accepted completely what we knew.

I believe that every Marine thinks that they are going to die, that it will be a heroic death, one that saves the lives of others. That, however, is a glorified notion, an abstract idea, a vague picture in the mind, a blurry image from a half-remembered movie. We want to save lives, but we haven't grasped what that will entail, and we don't want to grasp it because it may keep us from doing what we have to do. Knowing exactly what our dream involves will make doing it even harder. Well, we, the Marines of the Mortuary Affairs platoon, are the reality to that collective hallucination. While other Marines continue to carry around the dream, we clean up its reality.

8

Pushed

NEW YORK—*U.S. female soldiers in Iraq were assaulted or raped by male soldiers in the women's latrines, and an alarming number committed suicide, Col. Janis Karpinski reportedly testified before an international human rights commission of inquiry last month.*

"Because the women were in fear of getting up in the darkness [to go to the latrine], they were not drinking liquids after 3 or 4 in the afternoon," Karpinski testified, according to a report on Truthout.org. "In the 100 degree heat, they were dying of dehydration in their sleep."

The latrine for female soldiers at Camp Victory wasn't located near their barracks, so they had to go outside if they needed to use the bathroom, Karpinski told retired U.S. Army Col. David Hackworth in a September 2004 interview, Cohn reported. "There were no lights near any of their facilities, so women were doubly easy targets in the dark of the night." It was there that male soldiers assaulted and raped women soldiers.

Karpinski testified that a surgeon for the coalition's joint task force said in a briefing that "women in fear of getting up in the hours of darkness to go out to the port-a-lets or the latrines were not drinking liquids after 3 or 4 in the afternoon, and in 120-degree heat or warmer, because there was no air-conditioning at most of the facilities, they were dying from dehydration in their sleep."

From: "Rape Fears Lead Women Soldiers to Suicide, Death,"
Vermont Guardian, February 8, 2006

If the Mortuary Affairs Marines were to some degree ostracized, the two females in the unit may have been pushed further from the mainstream of life at the Camp than were their male counterparts. While there are female Marines, the subculture of the Corps remains strictly masculine. Values like physical strength and emotional toughness are associated with men and Marines. Values like brotherhood and the attendant belief that we are a "band of brothers," are thought of in terms of a group of men who are as close as those who share the same parents, not as an alliance of men *and* women, of brothers *and* sisters. The rules that regulate our interaction, that descend from and support those values, are those that emerged long ago, from a society dominated by men and a Marine Corps consisting only of men. All of us, including the females, dress in men's clothing, express emotions through men's curse words, communicate through their deep and curt Marine voice and their forceful Marine gestures. Marines bark to each other. They engage in PT competitions with each trying to push their bodies further than the next guy. The word "fuck" is inserted into any word or phrase at any given time. Even when an officer is present, this is the nature of the game, which gives it an official stamp of approval.

The culture inside the females' tents contrasted with that inside the male tents enough to remind the females that they were still living in a man's world from which the tents provided a refuge. Cursing wasn't as prevalent and the atmosphere was more relaxed. Much more of the talk was about relationships—with one's kids or parents, or with the staff sergeant one tent over. This last example would be discussed with the emotional interest that would have taken place in a college dorm among the classmates of a young woman who was carrying on an affair with her teaching assistant. While the men watched DVDs that glorified war and hypermasculinity, the women were glued to a season of *Sex and the City* episodes. Each episode would trigger long conversations about fashion—the latest styles of clothing and shoes—and the clubs in which it was modeled.

Outside the females' tents, on the base at large and in the Corps in general, the topics of conversation are men's topics—sex, usually, and cars or sports. The DVDs we watched most often were men's favorites, boys' videos, really, like *Super Troopers*. Eight months of *Super Troopers*. Two-thirds of an entire year during which we all, men and women alike, continually peppered our conversations with lines from that movie, testosterone driven, sophomoric adolescent boys' lines, like, *I am all that is man!*

The eight-count cadences that motivated us and coordinated our marching and running in formation, were created by and for men. Cadences like, *"Momma and poppa were lying in bed, poppa rolled over and this is what he said, 'Give me some! PT!'"* They are straight out of an amped-up masculine world, yet the women stomp and march to them too, alongside the men. And they march along to cadences like:

See the lady dressed in black, she makes a living on her back,
See the lady dressed in red, she makes a living in her bed,
See the lady dressed in brown, she makes a living going up
*   and down,*
See the lady dressed in green, she gives out like a coke machine,
See the lady dressed in gray, she likes to make it in the hay,
See the lady dressed in white, she knows how to do it right,
Another lady dressed in green, she goes down like a submarine.

In the Corps, we are told from the first day of bootcamp that we are not black or white or brown or yellow or red or purple, but green. We are equal. This is drilled into us. We are treated equally. We are all one. We are all green. But the green we march to goes down like a submarine, and she is a woman, like six percent of all Marines.

The marching and running cadences also served to maintain a way of life and a way of seeing things that encouraged even top notch Marines to be perceived as *female* Marines. Several were entirely offensive to the sensibilities of many, but particularly women.

> *See those kids over by the river drop some napalm and watch them quiver. Cause napalm sticks to kids! Napalm sticks to kids!*

Several of the specific exercises we were ordered to do reinforced the male dominated subculture, with even legitimate ones being sexualized. *"Hello Dollies"* had us on our backs, spreading our extended legs, like scissors, to the leader's rhythmic count, *"One, two three,"* to which we would shout, *"One!"* He would shout back, *"One two, three!"* and we would respond, *"Two."* This would continue until the leader decided to stop. That exercise was a different experience for the two women in the group than it was for the men.

Young men want to have sex and there is little preventing them from doing so in the Marines. Technically, a Marine is not to have sex with a subordinate, as that would disrupt the chain of command and call into question the motives behind personnel decisions. There, on the ground, during a deployment, that would create a mess. Otherwise, most Marines will try to have sex whenever they can, with whichever females are available.

A female not interested in these advances may keep her hair short and her cover on, go without make-up and decline company at lunch; she won't watch the DVDs and pretends not to hear the jokes. She shows no reaction at all to the pornographic image on the monitor and refuses to drink water after late afternoon so she won't have to walk alone to the head in the middle of the night.

But young women enjoy feeling desirable. For some female Marines, it's a pleasant surprise to suddenly learn that men want them. Many men. In the civilian world, weeks or months may have gone by without a hint of interest from a man. A seeming eternity of weekend nights out with girlfriends, afternoons alone in coffee shops, talking on a cell phone to let observers know that, yes, she does have friends. Here, that world is turned on its head. Here you are a movie star, a rock star, and a porn star all rolled into one. All the male Marines want her, and with a relentless intensity that makes it seem real, that makes her feel like the most beautiful woman on earth.

It's hard for a woman to resist the continual onslaught of sexual overtures. She's far from home, and maybe for the first time. She's experiencing the relative deprivation of life during a deployment. She may be surrounded by death. She is lonely and wants the acceptance of male Marines who see her as a second class Marine. Peer pressure is strong from other female Marines who are having affairs or who are simply sleeping with many men. She has been socialized since childhood to gauge her worth, to some extent, by the amount of attention she gets from men. The civilian culture from home, from the college campuses housing young women her age, is in her, including those norms that tell her that sex with random guys, sex without intimacy, is understandable. Not only does the masculine subculture of the Corps push her toward these encounters, there is a penalty awaiting her if she refuses to give in to the pressure.

You could push back on the system in small ways, but it usually wasn't willing to budge. It was like trying to push back the ocean with your hands. You could make the effort, you could *do* something, you could extend your arms and open your hands, lean forward and push outward, but without any discernable effect. You were *trying*, but you were standing there alone, pushing back on a huge social fact, hundreds of thousands of people big, and a couple of hundred years old.

I tried pushing back once or twice, but without success. Once, we were marching to the cadence:

Momma and Papa were laying in bed, Momma rolled over, this is what she said, Give me some, PT! Good for you, Good for me,

In relative terms, this lyric may seem benign, but why is the male the one who is taking care of (some need of) the woman? Why isn't the man rolling over on his side and asking? *Asking,* not telling or just assuming?

On this one occasion when we were running and I was leading the cadence, I transposed the genders. I fell out of formation and turned around and sang my own version. Instead of singing, "momma and papa were lying in bed . . . ," I switched it to, "papa and momma were lying in bed, momma rolled over and said. . . ." I placed the female in the more dominant role, and I changed up some of the other words. That sounds innocuous enough, but I caught hell for it anyway. After we returned from a run, one of the sergeants approached me and said, "Goodell, you know that kind of language is unacceptable."

"But it's acceptable for Marines to say that about females?" I asked.

"It's disrespectful," he replied. "These cadences have been around for a long time. Who in the hell are you to change them?"

Some of the other Marines chimed in and added that back in the old Corps they could chant whatever they wanted, without having to worry if it was going to offend some female.

How, though, could it be otherwise? Gather men together, young men full of testosterone, pump up their masculinity, remove them from the constraints of normal, mainstream society, away from their parents, their pastors and priests and rabbis, away from their wives if they are married or their girlfriends if they have them, and then toss a few young women in among them and watch what happens. If two women were assigned to a floor in a male dorm for the four years of their undergraduate education, would their experiences with men be unlike those of female Marines during a deployment?

It was as though there were two levels of asymmetric warfare being waged simultaneously. The first pitted the size and weight and technology of the Coalition forces against the relatively tiny number of underequipped insurgents. Lacking fighter jets and tanks and battalions of highly trained warriors, the insurgents fought back with suicide vests and car bombs, random mortar attacks and IEDs. They killed a lot of people and caused a great deal of damage but their greatest effect was political. They understood that a military victory was impossible, but that victory could be achieved by scaring the hell out of people and wearing them down and, finally, forcing them to question the viability of the course they were on.

The second asymmetric conflict was between the patriarchy of the Corps—with the traditional beliefs and practices that were embodied in many of the men who ruled the organization and that filtered down to the instructors who would too often set up females to fail. And eventually the word got down to the grunts in whom that message was reinforced. A small minority of the female Marines in their own small and random ways tried to mess with the system, thinking that maybe someone in power would notice or care or begin to make the changes that simple fairness and equity demanded. Or maybe they pushed back just to feel a little better for a short while. In either case, they did nothing so dramatic as blowing a seven ton into the air and making it and its occupants disappear. Instead, and individually, these few women may have changed a line in a marching cadence or named their Humvee *Noodle* and their weapon *Pork Chop*. Every now and then one committed suicide.

Mortuary Affairs bunker. Camp Al Taqaddum, Iraq, 2004. It was our platoon who filled sandbags and placed them on the roof. On one side the sandbags spelled: MA: NO ONE LEFT BEHIND *and on the other side it read:* HONOR RESPECT REVERENCE. *(Author collection)*

9

Fire and Rain

Marine commanders battling Moktada al-Sadr's
rebel militiamen in this Shiite holy city said
Saturday that the fighting had cleared the rebels from
the ancient cemetery in the heart of the old city . . .

The Marines described engaging in hand-to-
hand fighting in the vast cemetery, which lies
adjacent to the ancient Imam Ali mosque, a golden-
domed shrine that is one of the holiest in Shiite
Islam. The 11th Marine Expeditionary Unit, which
returned to Iraq recently after taking part in the
American-led invasion last year, had endured the
fiercest battle of all its engagements in Iraq, the
commanders said.

"The engagements in the cemetery were done on
foot, encountering numerous fighters at a range when
you can smell a man, and it's hand-to-hand combat,"
said Col. John Mayer, who leads the battalion that
took part in the fighting.

From: "Conflict in Iraq: Combat; Marines Pushing
Deeper into City Held by Shiites," by Alex Berenson and
John F. Burns, The *New York Times,* August 8, 2004

Mortuary Affairs was fortunate enough to procure a television for the bunker, which we kept tuned to CNN all the time. Also, Cotnoir approached The Sir to ask if we could play music softly while we were processing remains. Thinking it would be disrespectful, The Sir refused initially, but once the exact nature and volume of our work became clear, he relented. We played James Taylor just about all of the time. I had always liked Taylor and hoped to continue to, so I tried not to listen to his music while we worked. I tried to block an association between the two, but that proved impossible. It turned out that on those occasions when processing was particularly difficult, lines from his *Fire and Rain* helped.

In Tent City, the preference among the younger Marines was for the loud, discordant music with repetitive lyrics that were frequently shouted, a style often found in rap and alternative heavy metal. It wasn't unusual for a group of young men to gather around an X-box's built in screen to listen to a song while watching the accompanying video. A favorite was Drowning Pool's *Let the Bodies Hit the Floor,* in which scenes of soaring fighter planes, piercing missiles, and exploding tanks were accompanied by chants that *nothing's wrong with me* and *something's gotta give,* alternating with a count of, presumably, bodies hitting the floor.

Leaving Tent City for the bunker meant substituting the loud, raucous music that pumped up troops for battle, for the soft sound and gentle voice of James Taylor who was plaintively asking for the strength to get through another day, a day filled with loneliness, broken dreams, and flying machines in pieces on the ground.

One of our tougher days, the kind that the music helped us through, occurred after a platoon of Marines was on a security patrol. They were in a single file line with their packs and gear on, securing an area. When they finished they did a head count and realized that two Marines were missing. Marines don't go missing. They don't wander off. Marines do what they're told. That's who we are. It is good that two Marines are missing rather than only one. If there are two Marines unaccounted for, you know that both are somewhere together, which is better than if one were missing alone. The platoon sergeants alerted the men at the security posts stationed around the perimeter of the base. They were advised that if they saw two men with packs walking together, they were to hold fire. When nothing came back from the security posts, they called us.

An investigation charted the route the platoon had followed and we were sent out to find them. At one point the Marines were walking along the shore of a lake. Navy divers accompanied us, and soon enough they found the two. By the time they were pulled from the lake, they had been submerged for quite a while. The water made the remains swell. One man was so bloated and misshapen that we had difficulty carrying him properly in the litter. His neck was as wide as his bloated head and his stomach jutted out like a barrel. His testicles were the size of cantaloupes. His face was white and puffy and thick. Not fat, but thick. It was unreal. He looked like a movie prop, with thick, gray, waxy skin and thick purple lips. We couldn't stop looking at these bodies because they were so out of proportion and so disfigured and because, still, they looked like us.

We didn't usually look at the faces. Our minds would play tricks on us when we looked at the faces. We'd do minimal work on the face, only if there were a wound or a tattoo that had to be documented. Then we'd cover the face so we didn't have to see it anymore, so we didn't have to see the eyes. This time we couldn't stop staring at the faces, especially the one that was so terribly distorted. We could tell from his face that he had struggled and had experienced extreme fright and anguish. He had a look of fear. His eyes were swollen and his mouth was pulled back in a look of shock. The other Marine's face was calm. Calm as could be.

I interviewed their platoon members and documented their report but we still didn't know what had happened. I wondered how the two men fell into the water. All Marines can swim. We are all trained to swim. We are trained to save others and ourselves from drowning. How did these two fall into that lake? We knew that one of them fell in and was momentarily unconscious when the second jumped in to save him.

That's the thing about Marines: we completely put our lives in the hands of our fellow soldiers. I trust my life in the other Marine's hands. Not only do I believe completely that he's going to defend my life, I believe he's going to *save* it. One hundred percent. I know with 100% certainty that he is going to save my life and that if he does not, he is going to die trying. The source of this belief goes all the way back to the beginning, all the way back to boot camp, where each Marine made the decision to die for the Marine next to him or her, and without thought. It has to be without thought because when the bullets are flying, you can't be wondering about these things. This decision must already have been made. I know that the Marine, the calm one, didn't even bat an eye. He immediately jumped into the lake, gear and all. I know that when Marines pack their gear and go out on patrol, they're carrying at least 75 pounds. Our arms are through straps, our 782 gear is buckled around our waist, our flack is velcroed up. We are rocks. This man, without a thought, jumped in to save another Marine.

Processing these bodies was emotionally brutal, for too many reasons. There was the shock and horror of the physical effects of the water on the bodies, the sadness of knowing we were sending some parents' boys home looking the way they did. Yet, at the same time, there was pride in knowing that we were all a part of a group of human beings who were ready to give our lives for one another. And it's not just pride. It's accompanied by a crystal clear knowledge in our minds and a deep understanding in our hearts that our shared time here together is meaningful, and that meaning comes from our willingness to sacrifice for one another. This realization is something I wish I could have told the parents, spouses, and children of the Marines we sent home. I wish I could have said to the parents of one of them, "*Your son died knowing that he was valuable enough for another to give up his life to save";* to the other set of parents, I would have said, *"Your son gave his life trying to save another mother's child."*

Some Iraqis seemed happy to see American soldiers, while others did not.
(Photo courtesy of Bill Thompson)

10

Processing Iraqis

Four contractors working for the American-led coalition in Iraq have been killed and their bodies mutilated by a mob after their vehicles were ambushed in Fallujah.

Witnesses said the contractors' two four-wheel-drive vehicles were forced to stop before the mob set them alight with some bodies still inside.

The 150-strong crowd chanted slogans such as "Long live Islam" and "God is greatest" as one member of the crowd kicked a badly burned body lying near the vehicles . . .

At least two bodies were tied to cars and pulled through the streets while another was doused in petrol and set on fire, witnesses said.

The mob then dismembered some of the bodies and hung the limbs from a pole. Two incinerated bodies were later hung from a bridge over the Euphrates.

From: "Iraqi Mob Kills Contractors in Ambush,"
The London Telegraph, March 31, 2004

We processed the bodies of dead Iraqis too, as well as those of others who were fighting with us and against us and dying. It wasn't possible to identify the nationality by the body itself, and there wasn't always identification. After getting the remains, we tried our best to complete the paperwork, like we did with our own. We'd note distinguishing features, shade the missing parts black, describe the wounds, and so on. Often, the paperwork remained incomplete because there weren't tattoos, there weren't dog tags, there weren't driver's licenses.

Whenever we picked up Iraqis on convoys we showed respect, but on a couple of occasions we inadvertently stumbled. One time we arrived at a scene after a car bomb had exploded. Standing nearby was a mother and a father and their baby. I didn't go but one of the Marines who did told me about it. We showed up to pick up or clean up or to help in any way we could. None of the victims was American or coalition forces. The woman, the mother, was screaming frantically, wailing, pointing at the Marines' feet. A translator explained that the man was actually standing on the ashes of her baby. But there was no way he could possibly have known.

Another time we went out to pick up Marines and found a dead Iraqi man as well, and brought him back to the bunker. We notified the local towns that we had him and asked that the family come to get him, or, if the family preferred, we could bring him to them. We heard nothing. Nobody came for him. Days went by. We were getting other Marines to process and there was only so much room in the reefer. After twelve days during which no one came to claim him, we were told to bury him. The MA unit at Al Assad did the actual burying of Iraqis, following a specific procedure. The bodies were buried in long trenches, with at least 18 inches of soil between each body bag, and with each of the dead facing Mecca. After the grave was filled in, a Muslim military chaplain would recite the Islamic prayers for the dead. We would also mark the location of each body and keep a record of it in the event that family members eventually came to reclaim it.

In this case, that's what happened. Days after the burial, the family came to Taqaddum looking for him. We sent them north to Al Assad. The Marines there dug up the body, which they then sent back to Taqaddum to ensure that the paperwork matched the man. When the body arrived, we had to open the body bag to identify the body. It was . . . terrible. This was a dead body. It had been dead for several weeks. It had been buried. We tried to do for the Iraqis what we did for the Americans we processed, especially when it wasn't easy.

I remember hearing about a Marine who had an attitude about the Iraqi bodies we processed. He asked questions like, "Why are we processing these bodies when we are Americans and these are the people who we are fighting against? These might be the guys who are killing us!" Maybe we processed some insurgents but it's hard to say. If the body was intact but missing an ID, it could have been an insurgent. If it remained unclaimed, it could have been an insurgent. To us it did not matter.

That sentiment wasn't voiced again or by anyone else. For one thing, we knew plenty of Iraqis and, if they died, we felt responsible. For example, we had several Iraqis working on base, but slowly, after a couple of months, fewer and fewer of them came to work, then fewer and fewer still. One of the men from the restaurant who we had gotten to know wasn't around anymore. We were told that other Iraqis warned him that if he continued to work on base, they'd kill his family. He explained that he didn't have a choice, that he had to work, and he begged them not to follow through on their threat. When he returned home one night he found his entire family dead. He never came back to base. Other Iraqi employees were shot and killed by extremists for being associated with us. That tore at us.

We were all volunteers. We weren't drafted. We weren't forced to join. We all came to the Marines of our own accord. Mortuary Affairs itself was a volunteer platoon. If we didn't want to be in MA we could have walked at any point. No consequences. We could have walked right out the door. If it were too hard to do the job the way it had to be done, we could leave.

We saw on CNN what was done to the American contractors in Fallujah. We couldn't understand how someone could mutilate another human's remains and drag them through the streets. The stereotype has many people believing otherwise, but most Marines didn't go to Iraq to kill and maim. We volunteered to go to Iraq because we wanted to help, we went to change things for the better, to help make life better for the people of Iraq. It may sound self-serving, but that is the truth.

We processed enough Iraqis for us to build a room in the bunker dedicated to meeting the families who would come to pick up their relative's remains. The Sir handled that responsibility and was helped out by Cotnoir who had similar experiences as a civilian mortician. After learning that the custom in Iraq during a tragic transaction like this was to sit with the family members and offer them tea, The Sir managed to buy an Iraqi tea set. The Sir would sit at a table with the deceased relatives, at least once with the parents of a young girl killed by an IED, and, as the custom required, say, "It is Allah's will." I don't know where he found the strength, but he did, and we all admired him for it.

(Photo courtesy of David Leeson)

11

Toll

---

*The Department of Defense announced today
the death of three Marines who were supporting
Operation Iraqi Freedom.*

*Lance Cpl. Caleb J. Powers, 21, of Manfield,
Wash., died Aug 17 due to enemy action in Al
Anbar Province, Iraq. . . .*

*Lance Cpl. Dustin R. Fitzgerald, 22, of Huber
Heights, Ohio, died Aug 18, in a non-combat
related vehicle incident in Al Anbar Province,
Iraq. . . .*

*Sgt. Harvey E. Parkerson III, 27, Yuba City,
Calif., died Aug 18 due to enemy action in Al Anbar
Province, Iraq. . . .*

From: "DOD Identifies Marine Casualties,"
wwwdefense.gov/releases, August 19, 2004

The Marines of Mortuary Affairs, as tough as any Marines anywhere, cried. Usually, the tears would come when they heard from
home or were looking at the latest picture of their young daughter
or heard that their girlfriend found another man. But I'm thinking
the tears may have been caused more by what we were going
through in the bunker and on convoys. They also got physical. I
think the Marine Corp attracts men who are physical. Most haven't
graduated from college. Many, when they are pushed, get angry
rather than reflective, and tend to throw things rather than talk
about them. It wasn't uncommon for them to drop whatever they
were doing and walk outside. They may wreck sandbags or throw
their gear down to the ground. A civilian may throw his gear to the
ground and a safe assumption is that he's mad, but Marines don't
do that. Not only don't we do that, we are *trained* not to do that.
We're taught that before our rifle hits the deck, we hit the deck. If
a Marine deliberately throws his weapon to the ground, something
is very wrong.

We lost two men from our original platoon who said that they
couldn't, or wouldn't, do it anymore, and left. Our jobs seemed to
take a heavier toll on them. They ate less than the rest of us did, had
difficulty sleeping, and cried more. One would take a box of Nyquil
tablets every day and drink as much cold medicine as he could get
his hands on but that only seemed to make matters worse. He had
gone out on a particularly difficult convoy, to a tank that had been
blown up, obliterated except for the tracks, leaving thousands of
body parts—fingers and testicles and ears and pieces of tiny scraps
of tissue to be collected. It was shortly after that when I heard that
he was medevacked out.

Whenever the workload became too much for us to handle on
our own, Marines from elsewhere were asked to help us out. Most
couldn't hack it and left after one or two shifts. A couple broke
under the pressure and started doing what we all agreed was crazy
shit, and they were "un-volunteered." A Marine named Leslie stuck
it out, even though we nicknamed him "Nancy," seeing as how he

already had a girl's name. He didn't mind. He was a very funny guy who tried to introduce a degree of levity into *everything*, even this heartbreaking and frightening work we were doing, and if calling him Nancy gave us a smile, he was happy to oblige. He would, in fact, respond to a name we had hoped would annoy him a little, with a dance. He'd rotate his hips rhythmically while swinging his arms around in circles.

Even more disconcerting than losing platoon members and volunteers, was the fact that we all started hearing and feeling the souls of the dead we had processed and housed, as well as all of the dead killed in the Middle East since the beginning of religion, if not since the dawn of time. I heard once that the ancient beliefs of this region held that a spirit seeps out of a body that isn't buried properly or from a person who died violently, and that it hangs around for generations terrorizing the living, occasionally staying underground where it eats dirt.

In 2004, in the Mortuary Affairs platoon, that belief made sense. It seemed entirely rational to us when it was three in the morning and we were in Iraq, processing. At that moment and in that place, we were true believers.

There are many religious people in Iraq. It's the area mentioned most frequently in the Bible. Our bunker was close to the place where, we were taught, Adam and Eve were created, where the original sin was committed, where Christianity began, and where the devil himself once staked a claim and called home. We were taught that this is where civilization began, not far from base, right out there between those two rivers, the Tigris and Euphrates. It all felt so tangible. We could *feel* the souls of these civilians, and these mothers and children who died horrendous deaths. Their souls were on the land and all around us; they were in the bunker with us. Maybe what these people know about life and death, human beings and ghosts, was real, not just some hallucination. The line separating the living from the dead, once clear and indelible, became blurred. It often became even less distinct when we were processing remains. A string of lights ran along the periphery of the open bunker's ceiling, but the light by which we processed remains came from searchlights that surrounded our work tables. They sat atop five-foot high stands and projected our shadows onto the walls of the bunker. There we were disembodied, ephemeral, growing and shrinking in an instant, passing through each other, disappearing and reappearing again and again.

The bodies stayed with us until we shipped them back to the States after first stopping in Kuwait. The planes taking them back did so on an inconsistent schedule, requiring us to hold the remains for varying lengths of time, keeping them refrigerated to slow down the decomposition process. That was fine during the day, but not at night, when there were only two Marines on duty, and one slept while the other was in charge of refueling the generators that kept the reefer cool.

One night when I was the Marine who was awake, alone, at four in the morning, and, for security reasons, in the pitch black and without city lights to illuminate a sense of place, I could feel them. I was searching for the generators, in the middle of nowhere, when I felt the energy, or the spirits, or whatever it is you want to call the souls of the dead. I felt it like I felt the desert sun. It was that real. I could hear it like I heard the loud din of the generators. It was that real. It wasn't just me who experienced this; we all did.

When I was in the bunker alone on the night shift, when I was on duty and the other Marine was asleep, I'd hear the souls that we'd processed walking around. One night when I was in the front of the bunker, I heard the back door open and shut and then heard the sound of footsteps. We built the door with a weighted pulley so it would shut automatically behind us. We could hear it close shut, clearly, even from the front of the bunker. The floor of the bunker was cement which allowed us to hear the sound of rubber boots as people walked across it. It was very common for platoon members to come to the bunker at night because they would want to use the Internet or the phone and, at night, no one else was there, and there was ready access to both. When I heard the footsteps that night, I'd got up thinking it was my buddies. I was happy they had come by because I was getting tired and starting to feel sleepy. I looked around and there was nobody there. So I returned to the front of the bunker and waited for whoever it was who came through the door. I knew that whoever it was, they would come to the area I was in, where the phone and laptop were. I waited and waited, all the time wondering who it was and why they hadn't come to the front yet. I left the duty hut again to investigate and again there was no one around. I did a weapons count to make sure that all the weapons were accounted for. Then I checked the gear. Then I made sure that The Sir was in his rack, and that Sergeant Cotnoir and Sergeant Johnson were in theirs. Everything and everyone was where they were supposed to be. All the weapons were accounted for, all the gear was accounted for, all the people were accounted for. There was no way to explain what was going on. I returned to the duty hut and within minutes heard the footsteps again. But there was nobody there.

One time the base was on high alert because Intel said we were going to be attacked that night. The Sir called every Marine to the bunker and told us that we were all going to sleep there that night. There were five racks in the bunker which meant that ten or twelve of us would not have a place to sleep. After some discussion, several of us tried to sleep on the litters, which are like stretchers, and were what we carried the remains on. We set them up and some of the guys tried to settle in, but none could. Suddenly, one Marine flew off his litter as though he had been catapulted. He swore he had been pushed off. Strong, fearless, exhausted men, stood by their empty litters shaken and unable to get back on. We had an entire bunker to sleep in that night, but we ended up together in one corner. Grown men and women. Combat hardened Marines. It came to feel like we were living in two worlds or between two worlds, between the living and the dead. We were the living among the dead, living in their world more than they were in ours. We were the ones piecing together and shipping home the remains of the dead, but we were never sure what we were doing to the souls of the dead, or what they were doing to us.

There was a toll, no doubt, but not strictly in a bad way. Sometimes you pay a toll for privilege, like using a particular road or bridge. Well, a toll must be paid. We paid a heavy toll for what we did, but it was a deep privilege.

One day we pulled our Humvees and guidon out and the Marines took photos posing in front of them. Every Humvee carried a spare tire, and we attached A frames to the hoods in the event one broke down or was hit so we could tow it back to base. (Author collection)

12

Immorality Plays

---

*Documents I recently obtained show that the same
hostility found in the other services is deeply embedded
in the Marines . . . According to two DACOWITS
reports . . . women entering boot camp are told that
"there are only three kinds of female Marines: 'bitches,
lesbians, and whores.'" Both men and women say that
male Marines regularly call female Marines "bags of
nasties," or use the semi-official designation for
women Marines, "WM," to mean "walking mattress."*

*The men stated that women do not belong in the
Marine Corps. They laughed about the derogatory
names the women are called. One of the investigators,
Barbara Glacel, says that a group of men explained,
"in very graphic terms, that women should not be
allowed to go into any frontline situation because they
smelled so bad when they menstruated that they
would attract the enemy."*

From: "A Few Good Men?"
by E.J. Graff, *The American Prospect*, June 30, 2003

ACT: 1: Iraq. We're assigned partners for martial arts training and I'm paired with the biggest, tallest, stockiest male Marine in the platoon. I weigh in at 110 pounds, whereas he's closing in on 250. The instructor's rationale is that I need to learn to defend myself against someone bigger and stronger than me. Not only do I get my ass beat, but this bear of a man actually butts my face with the tip of his rifle, leaving me with a bloody nose and two black eyes. What I learn is how to take a brutal physical beating in front of fellow Marines. My audience learns nothing that they didn't already know: a female cannot fight with the boys.

Constantly reinforced, from the first day of boot camp to the last day of active service, this message was often presented in the form of a morality play. Orchestrated by an officer for the sake of the male Marines—for the sake of the Corps!—these brief performances shored up their basic assumptions about gender and war.

ACT 2: Fort Leonard Wood, Missouri. This is where heavy equipment diesel mechanics are trained. I am the only female in a class of fifteen. On this, my first day of training, the Sergeant notices me standing in his formation and screams, "Who the *fuck* is that in my formation? Don't even fucking tell me that's a *woman*! Get the *fuck* out of *my* formation! Get the *fuck* out of *my* formation!" I stand behind the platoon—separate and different—as the sergeant introduces himself to his men.

ACT 3: Okinawa, Japan. Only now am I told that I'll be participating in jungle warfare training. Everyone else is already on site. I arrive two hours late, just after the others finish rappelling down the broad side of a steep mountain. I'm at the peak's edge, alone with the instructor who is strapping me into the harness. I have the feeling that he *wants* me to fail. I sense that this entire scene has been orchestrated. Looking up at me from below sit several hundred Marines who have already descended successfully. I look straight down the steep mountainside through "hell's eye," a wooden frame through which I must lower myself before beginning a free-fall rappel. I'm scared to death but know that if I hesitate, I won't hear the end of it. Nor will the other female Marines back at the base. Nor will the next cohort of female Marines, one of whom, after being notified late that she will be joining the jungle warfare training group, will be brought to the top of this mountain, above an audience of male Marines, who sit waiting to see her fail. Nor will relatives and friends of the male Marines hear the end of it, even years from now, when, sitting at a bar in rural Ohio or lifting weights in downtown Chicago, they'll be treated once again to the story of the female Marine who was too scared shitless to jump off a mountain.

Here's how it seems to work. The instructors gather together a group of male Marines and have them do something "manly," such as fight each other or run an obstacle course or just shout out, in unison, in their deepest, most resounding voices. A female Marine is brought onto the stage and the men become an audience. The female is told to do what the males have just done. Take a huge male Marine to the ground or jump off of a mountain top or climb a long rope or run a fast five-mile course or rip the head off of a live chicken or shout a response to your commanding officer in the same booming voice you just heard the men use. If the female doesn't perform in the same way the men had, the audience's view of the world and the assumptions upon which it's based are reinforced. The Corps is a masculine world, defined by toughness and courage, and it admits females only at its peril. And at the nation's peril. Thus, the honor of the Corps and its effectiveness to protect the country are threatened by small, weak, fearful women.

Every now and then the plot of one of these playlets breaks down. Weakness defeats Strength. Villainy overcomes heroism.

ACT 4: Twentynine Palms, California. Our chief warrant officer is leading a platoon run. I am directly behind him in formation as the run begins. He takes off at a full sprint and I stay right behind him.

He speeds up and I remain on his ass. Occasionally, he turns his head to see how we are holding up. I look back too and watch as most of the platoon eventually falls out of the run. The chief warrant officer nevertheless continues to run, and at the same pace. I stay on him. Finally, he slows down and ends the run and walks over to the staff sergeant. I hear him complain about the men in the platoon. "Don't they have any pride?" he asks. "Goodell was on my ass the entire run. Why weren't they? Where the hell were they?"

An occasionally subverted storyline is not nearly enough to shift the entrenched worldview of the Corps as the quintessential male domain. The chief warrant officer didn't see any virtue in me. I wasn't hard working or persistent or courageous or strong. It was simply a matter of those men on that day fucking up.

From left to right is Corporal Sandoval, Corporal Clemente and Lance Corporal Goodell. The three Marines are sitting at the bottom of a ravine used for staggered seating during Jungle Warfare Training in Okinawa, Japan. (Author collection)

13

Personal Effects

---

*"One of the toughest things is going through the
personal effects," said Bill Lynch, 66, of Jericho, a
retired FBI agent who now works as a consultant.
His son Matthew, a 25-year-old Marine lieutenant
on his third tour in Iraq, was killed by a roadside
bomb on Oct. 31, 2004. Nineteen months later,
Lynch and his wife, Angela, only recently completed
the difficult task.*

*Sitting in a McDonald's near his office, the elder
Lynch picked up a plastic coffee stirrer. "If Matt held
this, I'd look at it and go, 'OK, what about that?'"
he said. "You wonder what is significant and what
is not. You emotionally weigh every item."*

From dailypress.com: "The Pain is in Personal Effects,"
by Graham Rayman, *Newsday*, May 29, 2006

I was sitting in the chow hall with a couple of MA Marines, not really eating, just observing Marines at the other tables. I noticed a man dab his chin with a napkin as he was leaving. I could see a spot of ketchup left on the napkin which he then scrunched up and put in his pocket. Then I imagined having to process his remains and catalog his personal effects. "One scrunched up paper napkin containing a red stain," I would jot down. It would be sent home to his family where his mother might devote the better part of a decade trying to make sense of it. *Why did he have a napkin in his pocket?* She would wonder. *What was the stain? Was it blood? Had he not died immediately? Was he initially only wounded but alive? Did he dab at the wound with a napkin? Was he in pain before he died?* She may be kept awake nights with a thousand unanswered questions.

This awareness became habitual. I couldn't see another person put anything into his or her pockets without imagining processing them and their belongings and sending something home that would only add to the family's pain. It felt like *I* would be adding to the pain. By this time it was summer and the days would get so hot that the sweat would drip into my eyes and the whole world looked beige except for the sky and sometimes it was too and then the sand would pick up and swirl and blur my vision even more until all I could see was Marines who would be processed. *That looks like a letter, but from whom? A secret lover? Mom? From one parent who is expressing negative sentiments about the other?* Occasionally all I could discern in the sandy mist was what was going into pockets, and then only sort of. Is that a ring? Who is that a picture of? *Are you crazy?* Or is it me?

I began paying attention to what was in my own pockets, what personal effects would be sent home with me when my time came. I got rid of everything I didn't want my parents to see and I was conscious of every single thing that I put into my pockets. After a while, I put nothing in them; they were almost always completely empty except for my rules of engagement card in my left breast pocket. What was in my wallet was exactly what I wanted in there, what I would want my parents to see and to remember me by. Everything in my tent was always organized and folded and cleaned or it was thrown out. I wanted to be an easy process and I wanted to have everything squared away for my mother and father. And I checked to make sure the labels on my clothing were accurate, so my parents would know that I had died if in fact I did. I made sure that no one else was wearing my clothes so that if they died my parents wouldn't grieve unnecessarily.

And from there I began to obsess about what I was putting into me, the type of person I was, and I felt an urgent need to square away that too, to square away me. Am I a good Marine? A good human being? And I reflected upon the type of person I once was, before joining the Corps. Were there people I had hurt and to whom I could make amends? What about that boy in high school who was a loner and who wanted to become my friend and who I ignored? I wasn't mean to him, but I chose to rebuff his friendliness and to avoid him. I wasn't unkind to him, but I hurt him and now I wish I could take that back, go back to that time and return his smile, say hello, stop and chat in the corridor. And what about the other loners and outcasts, the high school version of "fat nasties?" *Why had I avoided them? What's the difference, except for the matter of degree, between how I treated them and how we treat Marines here in the Corps?* I asked myself. But I also knew what the difference was: the odd Marine who was not sufficiently socialized into the group, who hadn't fully fit into his role, could get five or ten other Marines killed.

By June and July the temperature would easily reach 120 degrees or higher. The air conditioning wasn't always working and we would all sweat constantly, so much so that in the middle of the night, I could slap my hands down on the cot beneath me and the perspiration would splash up. The sand was *everywhere*: it blew into everything, covered everything, colored everything. The heat and the sweat and the sand together seemed to continue to affect my vision in that disconcerting way: I could see Marines putting things into their pockets that had no business being there. When I'd see such carelessness, I'd imagine them getting shot or blown up, and I would visualize what would happen to their bodies, and then I would mentally shade what was missing black. I would see that Marine in the chow line, the tall one, without a left arm and I would shade that limb black. That guy there playing soccer, a boy really, is missing his head, so I'd shade it black. This woman, in front of me at the PX, has nothing below the waist, so I'd shade it black. By mid-summer, everything was a dismal, sandy beige, or it was black.

14

Four Marines in the News

He [Professor Todd Gitlin] likened some war coverage—particularly that practiced by television—to a televised sporting event. Rather than journalism, it becomes entertainment. When the primary motive of media institutions becomes audience share, then these institutions 'seek a rapture of attention' in order to procure as many eyeballs as possible.

From: "Postmortem: Iraq War Media Coverage Dazzled But It Also Obscured," by Jeffery Kahn, *UC Berkeley News*, online, 18 March 2004

This is what happened. Our platoon received a call that there were Marines down and we needed to retrieve the bodies. The Marines were on a rooftop surveying a village for potential threats. Four men were killed. Three had been shot execution style, two shot through the eyeballs and another through the skull. The fourth had been shot multiple times and had his throat slit. Their gear had been rifled through and their weapons were missing. One Marine was found with his gear and boots off and another was lying on his side, covered with mosquito netting. Our platoon went up onto the roof to get these men.

By the time we got there, the bodies had been in the hot sun for a long time. The sun does horrible things to dead skin. It makes the skin slide off the body when the man is lifted. I wouldn't have thought that. I would have thought that it would be red and burnt. The skin actually detaches itself from the layer beneath and slides around on itself.

We took the four Marines back to camp and started processing them. It was difficult checking for tattoos and gunshot wounds because the skin kept sliding around. We couldn't grab hold and grip securely enough to move the remains, and we couldn't pick them up or lift them either, so we tried making slings. We put each body on a poncho. We grabbed and tugged and lifted each one in an effort to maneuver the bodies.

After several hours of processing the remains, we interviewed others, and pieced together two different theories as to what happened. Some thought that the Marines had let down their guard and allowed Iraqis to approach and kill them. Others thought that at some point the team went to two Marines on post while the other two slept, and the two who were supposed to be awake and alert and watching, fell asleep. We will never know what really happened, but in either case, Marines aren't supposed to get killed this way. It's bad enough when two men who fall asleep die, but then their buddies die too. In a situation like this, those on guard have the responsibility to protect those who are sleeping. That's how it works in the Marines. We are all dependent upon each other. We have got to be able to count on each other, otherwise, we all die.

It's not always known which Marines are on which rooftops because there is a certain degree of confidentiality involved in those assignments and patrols. Also, circumstance may require that a team move from one rooftop to another, and if the radios aren't working properly, it isn't always known exactly where every platoon member is. It's not written down neatly somewhere, so it was taking some time to verify the identities of these men. Eventually, I had the names of three of the Marines, but not the fourth. At that exact moment, when I was trying to verify the identity of the fourth man, I passed by the television and glanced at a breaking news story about this very incident. Apparently, video footage of the murders had been on Arab television and was being picked up by the news outlets in the States. The story's caption was "Four Marines found dead on rooftop," and what followed was a list of the names of the four dead men. I couldn't believe what I was seeing! If there was one person on this whole planet that's going to know these names first, it was going to be *me!* I'm going to know it first because when we broke up into teams to process these bodies, each team knows only the name of the remains of the individual they're processing. And because it was my job to compile all of the paperwork, I'm the only one who's going to know all four names, and yet here's a news outlet releasing what they say are the names of all four Marines to the world—and to the families?

What's more, and worse, is that the three names I had were not the same names as were on the screen. I couldn't breathe. People back home are going to believe that their sons are dead *when they are not.* Others will be relieved that their sons are still alive and safe *when they are not.* How can they be doing this? What's all this nonsense about fair and objective reporting? Would the men and women responsible for this travesty have done it if their own child's name was among the four that now were scrolling across the television screen?

It's as though the media needed a story and grabbed onto information that said there were four Marines down. Then they figured the story would be better with names, so they came up with names. I can't imagine where from. I don't even know if the names were those of actual Marines.

How can anybody back home know what's really going on here when what they hear often isn't accurate? Maybe the information is corrupted by the need of the news agencies to get a new story or a sensational or gory one that they can then glamorize, or, to get the story first. Maybe it's distorted by sloppiness or laziness or the confusion caused by the fog of war. Whatever the cause, the consequences are the same: a misinformed public, ill-advised political leaders, and families who are devastated.

Parents tried to protect their children however they could.
(Photo courtesy of David Leeson)

15

Mothers, Sisters, and Daughters

NEW BERLIN, Wis.—*With three daughters
serving in Iraq, John and Lori Witmer had a family
Web site with photos from Baghdad, notes to home
and messages of encouragement.*

*"Keep praying! They're almost home!" a recent
entry says. But the top notice, dated Sunday, carried
grim news: "We regret to inform you that Michelle
Witmer was killed in action April 9th . . ."*

*The 20-year-old private died when her Humvee
was ambushed in Baghdad, making her the first
woman in the Wisconsin National Guard to die in
combat.*

*Her family is asking the military to stop her
sisters from being sent back to Iraq after this week's
funeral.*

*"I can't live another year like I've lived this one,"
John Witmer told The Associated Press. "The sacrifice
that this family's made can never be understood by
someone who hasn't gone through it . . . It's a burden
I can't bear. My family can't bear it."*

—James A Carlson, Associated Press, April 12, 2004

At the same time that female Marines are sexual objects, they are mothers, sisters, and daughters. It's not a secret. If a female is waiting in line to use a phone, chances are good she'll be talking to her mom or dad. If she's leaving the Internet café, she probably just emailed a parent or a sibling. The care packages she receives are from her family. If she is a mother, the primary topic of her conversations when off the job is her kids. Moreover, this is how they are first known by the male Marines, before these men enter the military, when they are still young boys. Back then, as kids, they learned, to some degree and among other things, to perceive females as extensions of the women in their own lives, and to care about and to care for them, and to protect them too. And most of the Marines still feel this way. Not all of them, and, among those who do, not all the time. But many of them do. When the men are in this protective mode, they see female Marines less as objects to be harassed and more as mothers, sisters, and daughters to be protected.

A female Marine may fall out of a run early and not be verbally sanctioned like a male Marine would be. She's given a break, like a little sister might be if she can't keep up with her older brothers on a long walk. A male Marine may carry some of a female Marine's gear through the latter half of a 12-mile hump, and nobody says anything about it.

Even though The Sir wasn't much more than fifteen years my senior and was still a young man, he had a tendency at times to treat me as though I were his daughter. In the middle of one long night when I had duty watch, The Sir appeared holding a cup of hot chocolate. "Here you go, Goodell," he said and he disappeared back into his room.

Eventually, The Sir told me he didn't want me going out on any more convoys. "But Sir, I want to go," I said.

"I want you here," he replied.

I tried to reason with him, to persuade him to change his mind by reminding him that I was qualified to go on the convoys and that I wanted to do so.

"Goodell, we're going, you're staying!"

Marines follow orders, so I didn't go. I knew he was trying to protect me from several of the more dangerous and gruesome tasks that were assigned to us, and on one level I appreciated that and knew that my parents would too if they were to ever learn of his decision. On another level, though, it didn't feel right or fair to the guys or to me.

Pineda treated me this way from the beginning, and I was grateful that he did. I was more or less completely isolated and alone, though it was pretty much by choice as I just couldn't fit comfortably into any the available categories. I didn't want to give in to the sexual advances nor did I want to hang around with the women who did. In either case, I'd lose respect as a Marine and I'd have to put up with the daily hassles that accompanied either choice. Pineda recognized this and befriended me. He was not only my A driver, but he asked Sergeant Johnson if he could stand duty with me and process with me, explaining that it would be too difficult for me to do it with anybody else. When we did go out on convoys together, he tried to take on more of the gruesome work, leaving me with less. Once, when the base was being mortared, The Sir radioed Sergeant Johnson asking if we were all accounted for. When the Sergeant answered, "We're all up," Pineda asked, "What about Goodell?" He then spun around and ran across base—during an attack—to find out. Between mortar explosions I heard Pineda's screaming voice at the door to my tent. He was shouting my name. After I shouted back that I was okay, he turned and ran back to the bunker. He never said he was trying to protect me like a brother would, but that's what he did. Pineda had a sister and maybe that was why he was willing and able to offer me a much need friendship free of ulterior motive. Or maybe it was how his mother raised him.

I'm not certain what it is that transfers a woman from the first set of categories in which she is defined in terms of family, into the second that defines her in terms of a sexual object, but I think it might have to do with how well the men get to know the woman, more than anything else, and, then, with how good a Marine the woman is. As a rule, the men in a platoon will become protective of a female platoon member, especially if she does her job and does it well.

What complicates this already confusing system is that females may welcome the inferior role they are placed in by male Marines, especially if it is done as a way of helping out or protecting a weaker comrade. Just as men are taught to protect women in garrison, women are taught to accept that protection, and to find comfort in the knowledge that men are around to provide it, even if its underlying message is that women are weaker than men and that female Marines are weaker than "real" Marines. After all, it would be a relief to have someone carry your gear through the second half of a long run or to refrain from berating you when you come up with another sprained ankle that keeps you from marching. Even a cup of hot chocolate from home brings a great deal of comfort on a cold desert night, especially when it comes with knowing that a man with authority thinks of you, to a small degree, like he might the daughter he wishes to protect. But at the same time, it complicates things. Fall too willingly into a protected role and you look too vulnerable to be a good Marine and too weak and feminine not to be harassed.

The females who milk the system, who go over weight or sprain an ankle—again—don't have to run, they don't have to participate in humps, they don't get deployed, they don't go on training, they don't do anything, and the only thing that happens to them is that they are thought of as a "female Marine." Nothing is said about them except that, "Oh yeah, she's a female Marine. She's a female Marine, so that's what's expected of her. She's a Marine-ette." She doesn't meet your standards, she doesn't run, she falls out, she's overweight, she doesn't participate, and that's accepted, because she's a female Marine. That's what she is.

That perception of what constitutes a female Marine spills over onto all women in the Marines and it maintains a stereotype that then limits all women, even the good female Marines. These male Marines don't expect the female Marines to do anything, and they don't like it when they do. There are all these male Marines who dress up and play war all day and who lose sight of reality, of what's really going on around them. They don't expect the girls to pull their weight. So, when the *"girls"* can't participate for whatever made-up reason they come up with, well, the males don't want the *girls* to play anyway. They don't want the *girls* in their fighting holes, they don't want the *girls* on the humps with them, they don't want the *girls* in the seven tons with them, they don't want the *girls* shooting with them on-line. Because that's what they've been taught.

Improvised Explosive Devices (IEDs) quickly became the favorite weapon of the insurgents. They were easy to make, transport, conceal, and detonate. And they were effective. (Photo courtesy of Bill Thompson)

16

Boom

It is a grim reminder of the cost of war. But for Marines based at Camp Lejeune, North Carolina, getting a meat tag—a tattooed copy of their vital information inked into their skin—means paying a visit to Jesse Mays before they head off to war.

"They're used to identify a corpse. They're not for the living.

"Meat tags are so they can make it home," Jesse says. "No matter what. So someone can grieve over them."

Taken from information that soldiers wear on metal tags around their necks, meat tags go one step further. Jesse tattoos that same information on their bodies, usually on their ribcage just under their armpit.

"Flak jackets are amazing things," explains Lance Corporal Andrew Sichling, who isn't opting to get the tattoo tonight, but may do later.

"I understand why guys get 'em. If you get blown up, this," his hands frame his torso, "might be the only part of you that comes home."

From: "The Man Who Makes Sure Dead Marines Get Home," by Kristin Wilson Keppler, BBC World News America, Jacksonville, North Carolina

Improvised Explosive Devices (IEDs) quickly became the favorite weapon of the insurgents. They were easy to make, transport, conceal, and detonate. And they were effective. Artillery shells from the hundreds of thousands of tons of explosives abandoned by Saddam Hussein's military were hidden beneath sandy roadways or in animal carcasses or trash or discarded appliances or cars. Triggered remotely by cell phones, car remotes, garage door openers and dishwasher timers, they offered the element of distance and safety and, therefore, the prospect of detonating others in the future.

The explosions can be powerful enough to instantaneously erase a Humvee and its occupants. It can make a tank and its crew disappear, leaving only its tracks. The blast's shock waves send thousands of pieces of shrapnel spewing outward at astounding speed, and the gases created by the explosion can set a nearby vehicle or vehicles on fire.

The blast snaps bones and tears away arms, legs, and heads, shooting them up and away from the blast site, only to thud down into the sand tens of yards away, with the heads bouncing and rolling like so many soccer balls. They come to a stop wearing varying facial expressions beneath identical Marine Corps haircuts. The pressure from the explosion tears open air-filled ears and lungs and digestive tracts. Resulting fires burn and may incinerate the flesh.

While estimates varied—and they also changed as the IED technology changed—the consensus was that sixty percent of our injuries and up to eighty percent of our deaths were caused by IEDs. Most of the Marines we processed died from explosions. We would take classes on IEDs that were taught by infantry soldiers or grunts who lived among them and treated them with the respect they demanded. Many of us knew first-hand a Marine who was going home without his leg or legs or life because of an IED.

An artillery shell with a cell phone duct taped to it is an artillery shell with a cell phone duct taped to it. Whether you are an American or an Iraqi, a Marine or an insurgent, a four-star general or a grunt, that's what it is. Steel or maybe aluminum, casing and propellant, plastic and fiberglass.

It's the *meaning* of the IED that varies. To an insurgent, it may represent the power and perseverance of a sovereign people. To other Iraqis, it may mean that too, or it may mean a life of continuing uncertainty and danger. To the combat Marine in a Humvee or seven ton or tank, the IED is the ubiquitous unseen exit ramp to the unknown. To many of us in Mortuary Affairs, it represented an exit already taken, to a realm beyond life as we once knew it. That an IED's plastic is made from oil and its fiberglass from sand adds another layer of meaning to the device.

Ernest Hemingway wrote that ". . . in modern war, there is nothing sweet nor fitting in your dying." Written words, like an IED, can be interpreted in different ways by different people. After having seen and held the aftermath of modern weaponry's wrath, these words carry a particular meaning for me.

At one point we were driving through a village that was completely razed.
Houses were half-standing. Doors were broken off hinges. A ghost town.
(Photo courtesy of Bill Thompson)

17

Heads

BAGHDAD, Iraq—*Police found nine severed heads in fruit boxes near a volatile city northeast of Baghdad on Tuesday, authorities said, the second such discovery in less than a week.*

A roadside bomb also exploded near an American military convoy in central Baghdad, killing a woman and wounding three pedestrians, Lt. Thair Mahmoud said. The three-vehicle convoy was traveling near one of Baghdad's bus stations when the bomb detonated. The convoy kept moving. . . .

From: "Police Find 9 Severed Heads in Iraq,"
Associated Press, June 6, 2006

When we would go on a convoy to pick up remains, sometimes it was easier than other times, sort of. Sometimes it was a body and we would put the body in a body bag. Sometimes body parts were severed, but we could still pick them up and put them in a body bag. If it was one person, it would be easy. All the remains were put into one body bag and it would all be shipped together. Sometimes there was more than one person and the cause of death was an explosion. There would be many body parts and they would be strewn all over, all along the ground, and we would have to pick them up. When we were at these sites, often times, the remains were still hot, which meant that the fire fight just finished. Other times we would go on a convoy because they said they had a fallen Marine and we would have to wait for the fire fight to finish before we could even go in to retrieve them.

On occasion, we would scoop the remains by hand, scoop the flesh, handfuls of flesh, and place it into a body bag. We tried to get every piece of remains so that the extremists couldn't parade through town with whatever had inadvertently been left behind. We tried our very best to get every single remain.

Not all of us went on every single convoy. Maybe half of us went. When they came back, the half that didn't go processed the remains.

One time several Marines were killed at once and we had a slew of body bags flood the bunker. This would happen. There had been seven Marines killed and our Marines returned to the bunker with seven or eight body bags filled with flesh. We opened the bags and tried to sort out and organize the body parts and bits and pieces into coherent wholes. There was a foot still in a boot that still had a dog tag, and that went into one body bag. A leg, with that portion of the trousers intact that carried the Marine's name, was placed in another body bag.

Our goal was to separate and classify the remains in a way that resulted in the right body being sent home to the families, even though we all knew that, from the Marine's perspective, it didn't matter. If one of my Marines blew up and if I did too, we could be buried together. That's how we Marines are. We labored over this for the families' sake.

The Marines who didn't go on the convoy would never know what to expect when a body bag was opened. Anything could be found. One time Pineda and I pulled back the flap of a bag and found only mounds of shapeless flesh which we scooped out with our hands. Everything looked the same. There weren't four hands or a whole leg or a foot in the bag. It was all vaporized mush. We sorted through it all, doing our best to find anything we could identify that would help us.

At times we found gear in the flesh: Kevlar and an ammo pack and once, a radio. I pulled at a line that came up out of the goop, a phone cord with a receiver on the end. I untangled it from the mounds of liquidy flesh but couldn't remove it. It was stuck. Pineda helped me locate the rest of the phone inside the portion of torso itself.

We found a dog tag here and a blouse name tag there and color and texture helped us with sorting by race. Finally, we were able to arrange it all into seven portions, seven Marines, but we could tell we didn't have all of the remains, that parts were missing, though we weren't sure what.

A couple of Marines went back out to the vehicles to make sure that they had brought in all of the body bags. They found one more and brought it into the bunker. When we pulled back the flap of this last bag, we were looking into the eyes that stared back from severed heads. The bag contained only heads. We were not expecting that. At all. We removed them from the bag and placed each with the rest of its remains. We could tell they were all Marines. Their haircuts were high and tight.

By now it was almost impossible for us to look at the faces. We couldn't look at the faces anymore. The faces were looking back at us.

Certainly, we were always tired and we couldn't hold down our food, so maybe we weren't as sharp as we might have been earlier in the deployment, but the heads *were* staring back at us. We'd look away, then glance back to record any tattoos or scars or specific wounds or other identifying traits, and they'd catch us and stare us down. We'd have to cover their faces to process the rest of them.

We saw so much throughout the eight months of the program, and we managed to get used to a lot of it. A situation that may have made us throw up more or less continually early on, may have had the same effect only once at this point in time. But the heads worked the other way. They seemed to affect us more strongly as time passed. It was powerful and real and something we couldn't shake.

I sent an email to my mother about what was happening with the faces. Not wanting to alarm her, I was a little vague about the impact they were having upon us. I did, however, tell her about one Marine in particular who had been at the bunker for a couple of days and how I was getting a very bad feeling from him. Well, my mother assumed I was talking about a live Marine and offered me advice on what I should do to avoid him and how I should report him to the higher ups. Later, when I read her email, I saw mine to her below it and noticed that I'd addressed it to "Mommy."

18

The Girls' Generation

*Just two hours ago, Allied air forces began an attack
on military targets in Iraq and Kuwait. These
attacks continue as I speak . . .*

*While the world waited, Saddam Hussein
systematically raped, pillaged, and plundered a tiny
nation no threat to his own. He subjected the people
of Kuwait to unspeakable atrocities, and among
those, maimed and murdered innocent children . . .*

*When the troops we've sent in finish their work,
I'm determined to bring them home as soon as
possible. Tonight, as our forces fight, they and their
families are in our prayers.*

*May God bless each and every one of them, and
the coalition forces at our side in the Gulf, and may
He continue to bless our nation, the United States
of America.*

Speech to the nation by President George H.W. Bush,
January 16, 1991

Dark black-blue concord grapes thrive along Lake Erie's southeastern coast. It has to do with the hills and valleys, warm days and cool nights, and the Great Lake itself. A few miles south of this coastline sits the nearly twenty-mile long Chautauqua Lake, with its eastern and western shores almost touching at its midsection. The Chautauqua Lake area has long been regarded as an ideal place to raise a family. It has to do with the relative absence of big city problems, the close, generations-long ties among community members, and, perhaps, the persistence of small, organic, social rituals, such as Christmas and Memorial Day parades. These typically feature neighbors walking down the middle of Main Street, followed by a fire truck and a tractor-pulled wagon. Members of the previous season's high school football division champions, or Missy, the young girl from around the corner who won last summer's 4-H Dairy Princess competition, usually ride proudly atop the wagon.

It was here, a mile up the hill from Chautauqua Lake, where we lived in a comfortable middle class house, and where my mother stayed home when I was growing up. As a family, we spent many of our summer days on Chautauqua's gentle waves, boating, tubing, and skiing. My cousins and I enjoyed playing a version of "king of the hill," but without the actual hill. We had a raft with metal barrels as flotation devices which we climbed onto from the water, and from which my cousins and I would try to push each other off. In this hill-less version of "king of the hill," we would each try our best to establish sovereignty over our slippery, twelve-foot square kingdom. At the end of many of these halcyon days, we'd picnic on the lawn of my grandmother's house, with the waves lapping at our feet. Every Friday evening, regardless of the season, we would get pizza and wings and rent two movies which we'd watch as a family.

I played the piano at a young age. My father had played the tuba in high school and college and he somehow saw to it that I also developed a love of music. I practiced in the late afternoons as my mother prepared dinner. She was always preparing dinner, or breakfast or lunch, or she was baking cookies or cakes. When I'd hear

Dad's car rolling down the gravel driveway, I'd hop off the bench and hide. Our hide-and-seek ritual required that he, immediately after removing his coat, search the usual nooks and crannies looking for his young daughter. Only after some time had passed and he audibly expressed his puzzlement over where I could possibly be, would he spot my feet protruding from under the drapes, my hair falling out from behind his favorite chair, or my tilted face, with its eyes closed, sitting atop a pile of dirty laundry. In high school, I switched to the saxophone and played in concert bands, pit bands, jazz bands, brass ensembles, and a saxophone quartet. After each recital I'd hear my father's booming voice from the back of the hall shouting, "Great job, Jess!"

Soccer became my favorite sport at age nine, at about the same time that Mia Hamm helped to win the women's World Cup in 1991. Mia, the Michael Jordan of girls from my generation, was the proof that our parent's exhortations to greatness were grounded in reality. Mom drove me to my games, stationed her folding lawn chair close to the sidelines and cheered me on. Before the first half ended, my father's voice would roll across the field. "Com'on Jess, keep it close," he would shout, as I ran by tap-tap-tapping the ball toward the goal. The discovery that I was a competent runner led, years later, to a spot on the high school track and cross country teams.

The same summer I started playing soccer, I was the only girl on a Little League baseball team. I showed up to every game ready to play and I watched every game from the bench. The only exception was the one day I was put into a game for another player. I got to the plate once and hit a single.

Education was another value instilled in me at an early age. I studied, always did my homework, and, of course, read. And then read some more. A special emphasis was placed on math and science courses and I took to them easily. Though still a child, I decided I wanted to become an attorney, like my Dad.

"When I get out of law school, we can work together," I'd tell him, although it was really a request. "We'll call our firm '*Goodell and Goodell*,' I'd add, thinking I had come up with a clever name, or that he might have had in mind an alternative, like *Goodell and . . . Jessica.*

"Only if you're good enough," he would reply, "only if you're good enough."

The core of my universe fractured on the day my parents divorced, when I was sixteen. The familiar and comforting rhythmic patterns that were my life came to an abrupt end, though I was somehow able to continue the motions of everyday existence. During my senior year, I enrolled at Ithaca College, a small, upstate, liberal arts school a four hour drive from home.

In the spring of 2001, with high school graduation only a few days away, I sat with my classmates waiting to hear the bell signal the end of the period, when a uniformed Marine walked into the classroom and began organizing literature on a table in front of us.

"Why are you here?" I asked him.

"I'm meeting with a group of young men in this room in just a few minutes," he replied. "I'm going to ask if they want to become Marines." He emphasized that he wanted only *tough* men as the Marines are *hard core.*

"Tough *men?*" I asked. "What about tough *women?*"

"So you think you have what it takes to become a United States Marine, young lady?" he challenged.

"I know I can do what any guy can do!" I shot back.

Later that day, in the Marine recruiting office in nearby downtown Jamestown, I was shown color photographs of Marines in a wide variety of MOSs, or jobs. In one, an M1A1 Abrams tank raced across the sands of Twentynine Palms, California, with two Marines jutting out of the top, one from the turret and behind an M68 rifled cannon.

"That's what I want to do!" I exclaimed.

"That's not going to happen," the Sergeant said. "Females aren't allowed to be part of a tank crew."

After scanning photos of the other MOSs, I spotted a lone Marine, in the desert, standing beside a truck-like vehicle from which sprung a huge hydraulic arm at the end of which were two smaller forklift arms. I decided I would become a heavy equipment mechanic. I knew absolutely nothing about mechanics.

"This is it," I said to the recruiter, as I tapped the photo with my finger. "I want to fix heavy equipment."

He smiled and subtly shook his head as he jotted my preference on the form before him.

A face-to-face confession was out of the question, so immediately after enlisting, I called my father and told him what I had done. He said nothing. Not a word. I hung up and called my mother with the news. Her response was the same as Dad's.

Looking down a row of Tent City, which was built on the runway of an airport with each tent surrounded by sand bags. (Author collection)

19

Life and Death

The battle has taken a horrific toll. Doctors in Falluja say up to 600 people have died. The US military says more than 100 of its troops have been killed in combat in Iraq since April 1, many in the battle for Falluja. More American soldiers have died in Iraq this month than in the war against Saddam Hussein a year ago . . .

"I wanted to cry. It looked like a city of ghosts," said the doctor, who was too frightened of the resistance fighters to give his name . . .

—Rory McCarthy, *The Guardian*, April 24, 2004

The line separating life and death continued to blur. I would see the living as dead, as remains I was processing; and the dead were alive all around us, especially in our bunker. By now, Marines were returning to base talking of "ghost towns," and some were referring to fallen Marines as "fallen angels." McLaughlin was learning and sharing more and more with me about the land and its history and the widespread beliefs about its disembodied souls.

One night Bucket somehow got himself locked inside the reefer which was at that point full of remains. Apparently, he was in there for hours, and when he got out the next morning, he wasn't the same. He didn't look the same, talk the same, or act the same, and even he knew it. "Being in that reefer messed me up," he kept saying. "Way more than the brains had," he added, referring to the day a couple of weeks earlier when a Marine's brains spilled out of his head and onto Bucket's trousers and boots. We agreed, not doubting for a minute that there were spirits among us who were messing with us and who were most active in and around the reefer.

On another night, Pineda and I were assigned to process a Marine who had been brought in by his unit. We had the remains on a litter next to a table on which we had our supplies: gauze, dressing, scissors, face masks, and gloves. I turned away to start the paperwork and as I did I asked Pineda if he would do the fingerprints. He did, and as I was getting the sheet for the fingerprints, Pineda was moving the arms and working his way to the hands when he said, "Jess, something's not right."

"What do you mean?" I asked.

We were both expecting the man to be stiff. By the time we received most bodies, they're often "stuck," stiff with rigor mortis. When there's a firefight and a man gets hit, we can't always get to him right away. We have to, by order, wait until the fire fight stops and is broken up before we can get whomever it was who fell. If it is a lethal battle, it makes sense that you won't risk the lives of eight Marines to pull out one dead. By the time we obtain the remains, it's not uncommon to find that rigor mortis had already started.

This was different. Here the problem was not rigor mortis; it was the absence of rigor mortis.

"Look, I can move everything around easy. Too easy," Pineda said.

I glanced over and sure enough, the Marine's arms moved easily. Then, when Pineda let the arms go, they continued to settle. On their own. They didn't just fall back down, they moved, this way and that. We both jumped back and stared and for a moment I thought of what McLaughlin had told us about spirits in Iraq seeping from dying bodies.

I always pay attention to breathing. I always have, and I know I always will. It's when I can tell if someone is about to talk; I wait and I hear that deeper than normal breath and I know that someone is about to say something. I like to listen to the way people breathe because I know how they are truly feeling. I can tell if someone says that they feel a certain way yet their breathing is different . . . that their breathing is incongruent with what they're saying, then something's amiss. Instantly, I looked at the young Marine's chest and saw that it was moving and that the lungs were still breathing. The chest was going up and down, up and down. I spun around and hid. Without thinking, I scurried to the other side of the table and hid on the back side of the partition coming up from the table's side. We had built this work station with a section of plywood that ran the length of the back side and that continued three feet up from the table top. That allowed us to hang our tools and paperwork on the board. I crouched behind the plywood, peeking around it, staring at what was left of this Marine, and watching his chest rise and fall while his arms lifted with each breath. He wasn't dead. He wasn't dead and I didn't know what to do.

"What are we supposed to do, Jess?" Pineda asked disbelievingly.

"I don't know," I whispered.

In a moment, we regained a hint of composure and decided to get The Sir, who called the Doc, and the Doc said, "Just wait."

"Just wait? Wait for what?" I asked.

"There's nothing we can do," the Doc said. "Just wait."

"People don't wait for this sort of thing," I protested to Pineda. "What are we waiting for? What if this Marine were your brother, would we wait?"

The Sir and the Doc left and Pineda and I stood there for a couple of minutes that passed like hours, until the young man died. I couldn't process what had happened. *Weren't we Marines? Aren't we supposed to save every one of our own, or to die trying?*

I stormed out of the bunker. I just walked out, which is something Marines cannot do. If you're on duty, on post, you cannot just leave. Marines can't protest a commanding officer's orders, either. But I was so angry. And I was just a kid who two or three years earlier had been playing the saxophone in high school band. And I was so angry. And this was Mortuary Affairs. And The Sir had told us, on the very first day, that our job was a difficult one, and there would be times when we'd have to leave the bunker. As always, he was right: this was one of those times.

There are events that happened in Iraq that I will never, ever, forget. This is one of them. How could we possibly come to terms with an experience like this? And should we come to terms with it? If we were to, maybe that would mean that something was really wrong with us.

20

Anticipation

Camp Victory is located in northern Kuwait. The camp operation can redeploy about 10,000 soldiers every two weeks, which is also the amount of time the process generally takes . . .

While folks at Camp Victory, Kuwait's primary redeployment camp, deal with many of the same billeting and supply issues that affect the other camps, their job is made somewhat easier by the fact that most of the troops passing through the camp are on their way home and in high spirits. Living conditions are harsh. When sandstorm season began in 2004 its first victim was the tent over our Internet café, so communicating with loved ones back home was on hold.

Camp Victory
—Globalsecurity.org

Our six-month tour of duty was scheduled to end in August, but August came and went. Every day we'd ask Sergeant Johnson if he'd heard when we'd be leaving, and every day we were told he had not. Other Marines were beginning to rotate out of Camp TQ. Each week another group would pack up their gear and head to Kuwait. I saw Cherie—the corporal who had tried to befriend me—gathering her belongings together and I helped her pack. Now that we were leaving I didn't feel as strong a need to distance myself from her. I wasn't as worried about bringing her bad luck or about just bringing her down with reports of what was going on in Mortuary Affairs. I felt guilty as I helped her carry her gear out to the convoy that would take her away. As we waited together for a couple of hours in the heat, sand, and sun, I wanted to tell her why I had rebuffed her friendly overtures. I wanted to thank her for the opportunity I did not take to talk to her. I wanted her to know that I appreciated the kind of Marine she was, a straight-out top notch Marine, one who didn't hide in the role of a typical female Marine and one who, in a futile attempt to find acceptance, didn't try to pass herself off as a version of a male Marine. I wanted to tell her that in another place and time we would, I was sure, have become fast friends. Back home, we'd be college roommates, the kind who genuinely care for each other and who develop a life-long bond. A generation ago, we'd have been neighbors, each pregnant with our first baby, there to help each other adjust to a life at home. Instead, I chatted with her about the meals she'd have when she got back to the States, the comfortable mattress she'd sleep on, the relationship she'd enjoy with the man she was planning to marry. Suddenly, it seemed, Cherie was sitting in the back of the truck, wearing her flak jacket and helmet, waving good-bye to me as she disappeared into the sand.

They say that the most dangerous parts of a deployment are when you first get there and when you're about to leave. I could see why this is true. I could see the ignorance and naiveté of the incoming soldiers. They were way too careless and not half as serious as they should have been. Many didn't have a clue as to what awaited them. And for those of us who were about to leave, anticipating our departure made it easy to relax and to let down our guard. We were done being warriors. We had dropped our packs. We were ready to go home.

We got word in early October: Sergeant Johnson gathered us together and told us we were heading home. We went back to our tents and broke down our filthy, sweaty, sandy, smelly, uncomfortable, green canvas cots. We left the tents dressed in our cammies, wearing flak and Kevlar, an M-16 slung over our shoulders, each carrying two bulging sea bags, and a 75-pound Alice pack. We were taken to AGDAG (Airfield) and flown to Camp Victory, Kuwait, a huge base designed for transitioning into and out of Iraq, the base we convoyed out of almost eight months earlier. Now, it felt empty, like a ghost town. There was a skeleton crew working the chow hall and they were the only military I saw.

Our platoon was allowed to stay in any tent we wanted, so we all headed to a huge one close to the trailers that served as heads. There was not a designated tent for the females, so I slept in the same one as the guys. I chose a cot at the end of a row, between two other end-of-the-row cots that were occupied by the men I had come to trust most, Copas and Pineda. When I returned to the tent later that night after showering, I walked along the row of cots wearing a blue t-shirt and flannel pajama bottoms. It was a novel situation, and an uncomfortable one. For more than seven months these men had seen me only in cammies or PT gear and, now, I was walking past them in my PJs and with my wet hair down. I could feel their eyes on me. Nothing at all inappropriate happened and maybe that's why the situation ignited in me the faint memory of a complex sexual ritual more subtle and less crude than what I had witnessed since enlisting. It was a process that may have begun with the scent of a just showered woman, the hopeful glance of a young man, an averted gaze, a smile, eventually, a touch. I couldn't tell whether my recollection was from an old movie or a novel or a long-ago experience, but before my hair was fully dry, the memory became a promise of a future, post-military relationship of the sort I needed. As I slipped into sleep, the promise became a prayer.

We stayed in Kuwait for several days waiting for our platoon to be placed on a waiting list for a plane to Germany. A loudspeaker announced when a plane was ready for a particular platoon. Static and the word "Attention!" raised our hopes; the subsequent message absent a mention of us, dashed them. We were away from the MA bunker and the convoys, but we were still far from home. As time dragged, we felt we were in purgatory. Finally, our platoon was called and we humped all of our equipment down to the flight line. We stood in a line bordered by yellow rope, weighted down by our bags which we had to empty out onto the ground to show that we weren't taking back any weapons or other trophies from the war. We packed everything back up and headed to a second, nearby tent. We stood for several hours, then dropped our gear, then sat on it, then sprawled ourselves over it, to rest, then to sleep. The hours turned into days when, finally, we boarded the plane and flew to Germany.

From Germany we flew on a civilian plane to Maryland. We rushed out into the terminal, to the pay phones, to make collect calls to our families to let them know we were stateside, but to really let them know that we had made it home alive and, as far as we could tell, in one piece.

From Maryland we flew to California where we waited in a USO tent for several hours for the buses that would bring us to Camp Pendleton. There, we headed first to the armory to turn in our rifles. It was then that The Sir called us to fall in. We rushed to get into formation, not knowing why, but pissed nevertheless because we were home and the last thing we wanted to do was this. As we stood there, The Sir said "Goodell, front and center!" I marched in front of The Sir and saluted him, and he started to recite the standard promotion speech: "On this day . . ." he stopped, mid-sentence, saying, "Goodell, you know how this goes," and he pinned the Lance Corporal chevrons on my collar. "Don't go losing these this weekend," he added. The Sir wasn't supposed to be pinning me right then or there, but he had been trying hard to get me promoted throughout the deployment and could not. He decided to promote me anyway, thinking that after what we went through, no one would question him. It was a small promotion, insignificant, except to me. I was grateful. And I was proud.

The Marines of Mortuary Affairs, Camp TQ, 2004. (Author collection)

21

Home

Ken Dennis was fresh out of the Marines, finally out of Iraq, flailing financially and filing for divorce from a wife who ran off with a fellow Marine.

The combat rifleman wasn't sleeping much: nightmares. He had tried counseling but only briefly, then he had given up on it . . .

His best friend, Abram Hoffmeister, found him in the bathtub, a belt around his neck, blood vessels in his face exploded.

"It was pretty obvious he was dead," said Hoffmeister, best buddies with Ken since kindergarten in Ephrata.

Military statistics also don't follow soldiers home, out of uniform, out of the service, and into the stateside messiness of civilian life—a tricky territory planted with its own potential landmines: broken relationships, money troubles, legal hassles and mental stresses . . .

Ken's mother, Shirley Dennis, says her son's jump from military to civilian life was too quick. "There should have had more one-on-one talks with other vets. There should have been more realizing that you just can't kick loose these young boys after what they've experienced and seen."

From: "The War Comes Home: Rifleman Couldn't Take Any More," by M.L. Lyke, *Seattle Post-Intelligencer*, August 13, 2004

As we were leaving the bus in California, I was struck by the vibrant colors I hadn't seen in eight months. Other aspects of life, natural and social, that I had once taken for granted now seemed odd or wrong. And this feeling was immediate; it hit as we were exiting the bus. I could see vegetation and the air smelled fresh and clean. I didn't hear the loud chugging of the generators. Most of our friends and family members waiting for us seemed so big and round and colorful in their bright blue and red and yellow clothing; they resembled oversized gumballs that had escaped their plastic bubble dispenser, rolled to the base, and came to a stop before us. I saw smiles, hundreds of them, and toddlers and babies. And when I noticed husbands and boyfriends running to their partners with bouquets of flowers, I thought about this common transaction and its symbolism differently than I ever had before. Flowers for warriors! What does this mean? Who are these women expected to be now?

I woke up very early the next morning to join Leslie, the Marine who would help us when we got busy, the one we called "Nancy," for a run. He worked with us often and we all knew and liked him. He and another Marine shared sleeping quarters in a small room on base. It was still dark when I arrived and I noticed that the lights were on inside. Not wanting to wake his roommate by knocking, I quietly opened the door. There, taking up all of the available floor space, were six of my Mortuary Affairs comrades, arms and legs and heads, all helter skelter, over and under and around each other. These men had their own assigned sleeping places, but here they were, together, with the lights on, a litter of puppies, like the night in the bunker when we were threatened by attack. I wondered when the ghosts of war would loosen their grip on us.

Over the course of the next several weeks, I realized that many of my taken-for-granted assumptions about how we live here in America had been shaken by my experiences in both the Corps and Iraq. For one thing, it seemed that everyone I saw was eating. No matter the time of day or night, no matter the place, they were eating. They ate with others and they ate alone. They ate while driving and shopping and talking. They ate in restaurants and food courts, on park benches and city sidewalks, in elevators and buses, in movie theaters and ball parks. I saw a young man eating while smoking a cigarette and a middle aged woman eating while ordering a meal at a fast food drive-thru.

I noticed too how we were always buying things, and then buying more. New cars and then new stereo systems for them, and then new wheels, and then newer, more powerful stereo systems. Clothes. Jewelry. Cell phones that would soon be replaced with fancier ones. Flat screen televisions that would be replaced with larger ones.

Life was characterized by a carelessness that ranged from not using a directional signal when driving to not getting proper directions when on a road trip to failing to make reservations. There was a lack of attention to details that during a deployment could get people killed.

Everyone was busy. Too busy to meet, to have dinner, to carry on an actual conversation.

Everything moved fast. Strangers became best friends—"brothers"—or they became lovers—"soul mates"—in an instant. Relationships and marriages ended overnight. Jobs were lost, families were broken, plans were changed, and futures were canceled in the blink of an eye.

People seemed self-centered and relationships felt superficial. Favors were asked but seldom returned; everyone wished to talk and no one wanted to listen; plans were kept on hold until the last minute in the hope that something better came up; friends wouldn't show up or couldn't be bothered.

For a while I knew what it was like to have friends who would give their life to protect mine. Back home, I couldn't be sure that one would show up to an agreed upon lunch date or actually meet me at the library as we had planned.

Everyday life had the feel of a shopping mall, on Black Friday, and you were there alone, among total strangers, wandering around or, at most, transacting business. The Mall of America.

All of this—the rampant consumption, the materialism, the self-centeredness—the Corps had purged from us; then we were dropped back into the middle of it all. The experiences of war, of combat and death, left us jittery in public places, jumpy at the sound of fire crackers, sleepless at night. And it was these changes in what we saw as important, in who we were, in how we lived, in the bonds that connected us, or didn't, that created deeper problems in adjusting back to our old lives.

To say that this set of fundamental changes created a sense of confusion is to minimize our sense of the term "confusion." We did get disoriented with regard to time and, certainly, identity, but it wasn't just all in our minds. The disorder was also in our lives, in our interactions, our relationships, as well as in their absence. As we were soon to learn, the confusion was in the very ground beneath our feet that would give way like loose sand whenever we tried to propel ourselves forward, trying to get back to a source of social gravity, where life had meaning and our interactions had structure.

Before we left Camp TQ, every Marine was told to see a counselor. This soldier gave us each an electronic stylus-like device with which we completed a questionnaire, and then he called us into his office individually where we were asked the same questions. The same idiotic questions. Questions like, "How is your libido?"

"Well, we're in Iraq, in wartime, and I'm working in Mortuary Affairs," I said. After a brief pause I asked, "Under these circumstances, what libido?"

"I know where we are," he said, "and I know where you're working. What I'd like to know is how your libido is doing."

"Well, maybe someone could ask me when we're back in the States and things are more normal," I suggested.

"Alright, then," he continued, "How's your appetite?"

"Umm . . . the trucks that deliver our food to the base keep getting blown up, so now we're down to one meal a day. And I work in Mortuary Affairs."

"Okay," he said with a sigh as he jotted down my answers on his yellow notepad, "what about your sleeping patterns?"

"The base is under threat of attack every night . . . and I work in Mortuary Affairs," I murmured impatiently. When he saw that I couldn't hide my irritation, he directed me to someone else.

The second soldier asked the same stupid questions and then recommended that when I return to the States I should talk with still another counselor.

"Goodbye," he said as he extended his hand.

"Thanks," I replied as I shook his hand.

And that was that.

There was no debriefing. There was no attempt to communicate with us in a therapeutic way, or to encourage us to talk to each other. There was no nothing. Nope. Nothing. He just recommended that I talk to someone when I get back. He didn't tell me what to tell my sergeant when he'd say, "It's tough luck if you have to talk to someone, we've got things we have to do this afternoon." The counselor didn't recommend what I do then.

He didn't tell us that what we saw and did in Iraq we'd never forget. He didn't say that the images would keep us awake all night in a sweat or that we'd never fully rid ourselves of the smell of death or that we wouldn't be able to eat or leave our parents' house or our own apartments for months or that we'd shoot at neighborhood kids from our windows or pop sixty pills a day or wander the streets of our hometown in a stupor. The counselor didn't tell us that whole spheres of our lives and basic aspects of our selves were gone. Obliterated. That friends and family members and spouses, good memories, sleep, fun, food, and clarity would all have to be shaded black. He didn't tell us that for several of us, our former lives would be shaded black. The counselor didn't say that for a couple of us, hope would be shaded black.

*We received a call one day and were told that an IED exploded under
an Army convoy that was crossing a bridge. It blew a truck over the side
and down into a ravine. (Photo courtesy of Bill Thompson)*

22

Miguel*

In her study, Dr. Dobie and her colleagues mailed surveys to 1,935 women [veterans] . . .

The women who screened positive for the [Post traumatic Stress] Disorder also reported more psychiatric problems, more issues with substance abuse, and more lifetime exposure to domestic violence. They also had more physical health problems . . .

From: "Female Veterans Increasingly Diagnosed with PTSD,"
by Ruth SoRelle, *MPH Emergency Medicine News*,
Volume 26, Issue 6, June 2004

*Not his real name.

Before heading to Iraq, I did a two-year stint in Okinawa, Japan. From Okinawa I was sent to Twentynine Palms, California. Upon arrival another Marine took me around the base to "check-in," which involved getting assigned an M-16 at the armory, stopping by BAS and the Dental clinic, and picking up the gear that was issued to me, such as the Alice pack, ammo pouches, canteen, Kevlar and flak jacket. The Marine's name was Miguel. He was 6' 2' and 230 pounds of solid ox muscle. Hispanic and bilingual, Miguel had dark hair and eyes, and thick, solid, working hands.

Miguel and I started seeing each other almost immediately. We loved watching movies and spent many evenings doing just that at theaters, drive-ins, and back at the base. Soon, we were having all of our meals together, occasionally at the chow hall and often at the nearby Kentucky Fried Chicken and Denny's. We tried making a meal in the barracks once by microwaving macaroni and cheese and tapioca pudding, but spent more time cleaning up the mess than eating it. I didn't know that rented DVDs and fast food could feel so good, and for those three months I was happy.

I brought a picture of Miguel—in which he was sporting his straight-from-the-barrio "thug" facial expression—to Iraq and was quick to show it to those men who suggested we have an affair or a night of sex. In a situation like this, some men backed off to respect the relationship a woman was in. Others did so to honor a fellow male Marine. Many found their sex drive dampened by the sight of a muscular, angry-looking young man scowling at them from a cell phone. I emphasized the seriousness of our relationship by wearing Miguel's dog tags around my neck, until I became convinced that my own death was imminent and Miguel's tags would cause both sets of parents unnecessary grief.

Miguel visited for a weekend shortly after my return from Iraq, and within a month we began looking for a place to live off base. At this point he was about to end his active service while I had several months left. We found a tiny, 350-square-foot house ten miles from base. His parents were kind enough to give us a very used bed and dresser that they had purchased at a swap meet, and we bought the dishes and pot holders and whatnot needed to set up a small home.

Though he tried, Miguel could not find a job, and before long he showed a side of himself I didn't know existed. He screamed at me and threatened me and scared me. The man was huge and his rage seemed uncontrollable. I would cower, unable to move except for my trembling. One night he threw a clock at me. It was a large clock that had the poem "Footprints" enclosed in its glass case. The glass broke against my body and shattered over and around me. I was wearing shorts and a tank top and was barefoot. Miguel was screaming at me to get up, but I couldn't move. On another night he decided that we should split up between us everything we owned. I could hear him shouting loudly as he walked out behind the house to the shed, and when he returned I could see from my hiding place that he was carrying an ax. Yelling, he announced that he would chop everything in the house in half, starting with the dresser and bed. I scurried out from hiding and begged him to not go through with it and eventually he dropped the ax.

Miguel took part in the initial Marine invasion of Iraq in March of 2003. Assigned to an MP (military police) platoon that was in charge of the POWs, his job was to collect and re-locate those captured to detainment camps. The MPs hog-tied the POWs with zip ties and threw them into a transport vehicle and tossed them back out when they arrived at the camp. Miguel said it wasn't unusual for a shoulder or collar-bone or rib to break what with all the throwing around. Whenever I tried talking to Miguel about my Iraqi experiences, he refused to listen. He'd point out that because I wasn't part of the initial invasion, I didn't participate in the "real" war. My time in Iraq wasn't even "war-like," so I should just stop complaining.

Though no longer in Iraq I was unable to gain weight or sleep well or relax. As the stress became prolonged, I grew certain that I could get my life back on track if I were free of Miguel, and I was equally certain that I could not.

Support Our Troops. (Photo courtesy of Franklin Veaux)

23

Searching

---

*In 2003, I left the Marine Corps to pursue a career
and a life as a civilian. After numerous combat
deployments, a wall full of awards, and a chest full
of medals, I figured I could just walk into whatever
company I so chose and they would be blessed by my
leadership and hard charging motivation.*

Yea, right

*My first job was selling insurance door to door.
My second job was Starbucks. My third job—and
this is the straw that broke the camel's back—was
waiting tables in a pancake restaurant. Turns out
that the Corps did next to nothing to prepare me for
the "real world"—chaotic, unfair, undisciplined,
and unforgiving. . . .*

From: "Surviving Civilian Life: Part 1,"
Modernmarinecorps.com, October 6, 2010

My last day as a Marine was a normal workday, but when we were dismissed from formation at 1630 the platoon was called into the office where the sergeant said a few words about how I was a good Marine, then he shook my hand and walked away so that the real good-byes could be said. My friends gave me a plaque, which is customary when a Marine EAS's, or ends active service. We hugged, and then I walked out to where Miguel was waiting for me in his "baby," a custom painted Impala. The car—silver on the bottom, light green on the top half, and layered with five coats of gloss—was filled to the brim with our belongings and our new yellow lab puppy, Grizzly. We were headed east looking for a new life. Neither of us could live alone so we chose to live with each other, with another Marine, someone tough, who could pull their own weight, and yours too if need be. Someone with Marine Corps values who would watch your back, even save your life while giving his own if circumstances required—like the two Marines we pulled from the lake back in Iraq. Together, it was as though we had left the Corps, but not really, not entirely.

We stopped at the Grand Canyon. The views took my breath away and temporarily cleared my head. For a moment I forgot about where I had been and what I had done and was mesmerized by the vast expanse of the canyon. I wondered what was in there—in the rock and in its history—that we couldn't see. What mysteries did it hold? Miguel actually climbed out onto a ledge, and then lowered himself down several feet into the chasm to take pictures.

We left the Canyon and headed north toward Utah, enjoying breathtaking, panoramic views of a landscape dotted by huge golden rocks atop deep red sands. We traveled through this spectacular scenery for hours on end without seeing another soul. The highway stretched into the horizon like an endless ribbon, winding up and down mountain roads through rocks and dust and hills. When night began to fall, we pulled into a roadside motel and ate next door at an old Indian diner. Later, we took Griz for a walk until we found ourselves so far in the middle of nowhere that we were engulfed in utter silence, except for faint wailing sounds in the distance. Miguel thought it was the wind whipping through jagged mountainsides and fissured ground. To me, the noise sounded like human cries, especially when I remembered the Indian graveyard we had passed earlier in the day. When even Grizzly got scared, I decided that my interpretation was the correct one.

The next day we headed towards Goosenecks, Utah. We stopped only long enough to step out of the car and peer in awe into the deep, winding crevice scarring the earth. Its depth was surprising and its colors so vibrant and beautiful. We drove on to Mexican Hat, a rock formation that looks like a huge sombrero sitting in the middle of nowhere, as if it were once taken from the head of its giant owner and alighted atop a large rock. Long hours of driving passed mostly in silence, broken by conversation that revolved around Grizzly. It was hard to pick up radio stations, so for much of the ride we listened to my old Diamond Rio CDs.

We'd frequently pass vehicles displaying the yellow ribbon "support-our-troops decal," but we never once mentioned it. We probably passed a hundred or more decals—two hundred if you count the multiple decals decorating the cars of the more patriotic motorists—and yet neither of us even once said, "Look, more support from the citizenry. Let's give the 'thumbs up' as we pass." We didn't even say, "Look, another decal." We didn't even point. I'm not sure why Miguel ignored them, but I assumed he felt the same way I did. I knew that these people on their way to work or home or dinner had no idea what it was they were supporting. They did not have a clue as to what war was like, what it made people see, and what it made them do to each other. I felt as though I didn't deserve their support, or anyone's, for what I had done. No one should ever support the activities in which I had participated. No one should ever support the people who do such things. Plus, the yellow ribbons tended to be displayed by drivers who were hard-working, church-going, family men and women. They were the people we wanted to be. They had the lives we believed in and fought for and wanted for ourselves. But here we were, having all we could do to get up in the morning and act half normally. Here we were, behind them, with our belongings in the back seat and gruesome memories flashing randomly in our heads. Here we were, leaving the ribbons behind us as we sped up on our way to Hell, probably, where we would pay for the sins these magnetic decals endorsed. There was an irony of sorts shaping the dynamic between our ribbon decal supporters and us. They were uninformed but good people, the kind whose respect we would welcome—if it were based upon something true. It was when we were around them that we had to hide the actual truth most consciously. It wasn't enough to not mention the war or being a veteran, because they'd bring it up after noticing the Twentynine Palms decal on the car windshield or Miguel's haircut. They'd extend a hand—but only to him, as the thought that I might have been a Marine didn't occur to them, despite the vacant look that had already begun to settle behind my eyes—and say, "thank you for your service." And then we were in a bind. So, as it happened, the civilians we were most anxious around, and therefore tended to most avoid, were exactly those good citizens who thought they were helping us.

From Mexican Hat we headed to the Four Corners, which is where the states of Colorado, Arizona, New Mexico, and Utah meet. I expected so much more than what we found. We were, again, in the middle of what most would think of as "nowhere," on a stretch of lonesome road along which sat several stands selling inexpensive Indian jewelry, purses, and artwork. I wondered if this is what would one day become of Iraqi culture, if a hundred years from now, men in their white dishdashas and women in black hijabs would be relegated to roadside stands selling cheap imitations of a life long gone. On the exact spot where the states touched there stood an unremarkable cement slab, next to which I posed with Grizzly to have our picture taken. Then we hit the road again.

The following day we were cruising across New Mexico's desert with nothing at all in sight in any direction. We were, though, able to pick up a radio station and were listening when a song by Neo came on. I said, "I love Neo." That was that. Miguel was instantaneously furious with me for expressing my "love" for anyone other than him. "Yeah, well I love Paris Hilton! How does that make you feel?" He fumed and drove for a mile or so then pulled the car over to the side of the road, screamed "Get the *fuck* out of my car," tossed me from the vehicle like I was one of his Iraqi detainees, a prisoner of war, and took off. It was bright and sunny and hot. There wasn't any water around, anywhere. There wasn't any cell phone reception. I didn't have a map or any idea as to how I'd get to the next town. If gazing into the Grand Canyon momentarily took me away from Iraq, this put me back into the middle of it, but in this version, *I* was the lone pedestrian, strolling along a barren landscape, close to nothing, lost. That sole Iraqi man the convoy sped by a year earlier had to have been scared, I now realized. Eventually, I noticed a car on the horizon heading my way. It was the Impala.

Our next stop was Amarillo, Texas. We made Amarillo a destination because of a restaurant Miguel had heard about from a fellow Marine. The Big Texan Steak Ranch was a sprawling dining hall with a cowboy theme. It featured a staff dressed in Western gear, stuffed wild animals (bison and deer heads, a huge bear ready to attack), snakes (to view in their cages or to eat), and a video shooting gallery. We were drawn to The Big Texan by its "world famous" steak-eating contest, which Miguel was certain he could win. To do so, he would only have to consume a salad, dinner roll, shrimp cocktail, baked potato, baked beans . . . and a 72 oz. steak, along with a beverage to wash it all down. Making the challenge even easier was the fact that he'd be given a full sixty minutes to enjoy the meal. The contest was one Miguel would probably have taken on even if there were no external incentive, but there was one: once victory was his, he'd be given a Big Texan mug and t-shirt and the meal itself would be free.

Miguel was seated at a red-table-clothed dais flanked by a

gigantic digital clock. The chef came out to the table and, under his supervision, Miguel was allowed to taste the steak to ensure it was cooked to his satisfaction. He swallowed the bite of steak, reflected for a moment, nodded, and the battle was on. I was sitting in a nearby booth rooting him on, trying not to look at the four-and-a-half-pound slab of charred meat, but wanting to be the dutiful girlfriend-cheerleader. He started strong, but slowed and lost the verbal support of the nearby diners, and stopped before he could finish. We left stunned and empty-handed except for the $100 check.

We put Grizzly into a laundry bag the next morning, ran him out to the car hoping the staff wouldn't catch us violating their no pets policy, and continued driving eastward, into the bright yellow sun.

Grizzly and me at a state park near Twentynine Palms, California. (Author collection)

24

St. Louis

What got in his head? Former Marine died one
year ago after mixing heroin and Xanax.

A year ago today, Eric R. Jines died.

Twelve days shy of his 23rd birthday, Eric
died in a hospital emergency room suffering acute
respiratory arrest—the result of mixing heroin with
the anti-anxiety drug Xanax . . .

Eric's death ended a trajectory that had carried
him from early graduation so he could join the
Marine Corps, to combat in Iraq and to a return
home, where he struggled to readjust to the civilian
world . . .

His struggle was intensified by a severe case of
post-traumatic stress disorder (PTSD), a psychiatric
disorder linked to life-threatening experiences. Its
symptoms include nightmares, flashbacks, depression,
anxiety and mood swings.

After a year of grieving, Jines, a dentist who
practices in St. Louis, plans to speak next week to

an assistant U.S. attorney in hopes of launching an investigation into whether Eric obtained the heroin that killed him at the VA Hospital at Jefferson Barracks in south St. Louis County.

When Eric came home from Iraq in October 2005, he refused to talk about his experiences with the 1st Marine Division, Jines said. "Absolutely, when he came back he was so clammed up, he wouldn't say a thing. You wouldn't know he was in the Marines except for the tattoos he had," Jines said.

"I think it was the guilt he felt," said Eric's mother, Laura Jines. "I tried to get him to talk to somebody. I do think it was the guilt he felt for whatever he did."

—Mike Fitzgerald, *Belleville News-Democrat,* Dec. 6, 2009

Who knows how it was that we decided to live in St. Louis, Missouri. Neither of us had been there. We didn't know anybody there. We didn't have jobs waiting for us there. We weren't life-long Cardinals' fans. But there we were, in St. Louis, the Gateway to the West. Waking up at seven every morning, we dressed ourselves in casual business clothes, and scoured the city for jobs, with each of us submitting at least three or four applications a day. We talked to a kind, elderly woman at a Wackenhut security office and were offered jobs as security guards. Miguel got to work days, armed, for $12 an hour. I was told they'd let me work third shift, unarmed, for $9 an hour. I had a green belt in martial arts, one level higher than his grey belt; we were both expert marksmen; I EASed with a higher rank than him, but none of it mattered. Miguel took the job while I continued my search for a week or so more, until I found employment with a company that sold equipment to machine shops around the country. Shops would call us for parts when theirs broke down. My job was to answer the phone and type the order information into the computer. I probably got the job because of my background as a diesel mechanic. If a caller asked for an O-ring or a level or a gasket, I knew what he was asking for and was often able to help identify the exact part and send out the right one quickly. And I probably got the job because I was female.

I liked working at the machine equipment supply company. It was easy and fun. The other six girls in the business' front-end office were friendly and polite to me. The walls surrounding our work cubicles were low enough for the gab and gossip to flow freely and uninterrupted. The chatting would continue during the breaks in the lunchroom we shared with the warehouse workers and in which the television played what seemed to be an endless loop of *COPS* reruns and episodes of *Judge Joe Brown*. I began to make friends.

One weekend, Miguel and I joined one of my co-workers and her boyfriend and attended a car show in downtown St. Louis. Another girl, Shanna, would host a girls' night at her place on Tuesday nights, the night her boyfriend worked late at Best Buy. We'd watch movies and exchange recipes. Still, Miguel would scream at me as I'd leave our apartment to head to Shanna's, accusing me of carrying on an affair behind his back.

We split the bills down the middle, 50/50, but I did everything around the apartment—making us a big breakfast every morning, lunches to take to work, and a full dinner each night. I'd bake muffins and cookies and send them to work with Miguel for his co-workers. I did the vacuuming and the laundry and I cleaned the bathroom. I tried to be the ideal girlfriend. Despite the continued abuse, I sensed that life was improving. Or maybe I was just hoping it was.

I feared Miguel and knew that he was capable of hurting me physically, but I believed in his fidelity to me. My trust was implicit. It was the trust of a heart not yet irrevocably damaged by the selfishness of a lover. And it was a trust fortified by the fact that we were both Marines, tied to each other with a bond closer than that of brothers, by a willingness to sacrifice our life for that of the other. *Semper fidelis!* And so when Miguel asked me to get his credit card from his wallet for an online purchase he was making, I thought nothing of the post-it note that had a telephone number and the name *Monica* written on it. I mean he just moved across country with me and we were fellow Marines! I joked with him: "Oh, some girl named Monica has it for ya, huh?"

When he replied that I knew Monica, that, in fact, I had met her, that Monica was the woman at Wackenhut who had given us our job applications, my heart skipped a beat and my breath spewed out of me. That woman was in her seventies. Grand-mothers—never mind great grandmothers—aren't named *Monica*.

Fear, uncertainty, and pretense marked the following few weeks. I pretended to believe Miguel's lies even as I grew less cer-tain of what the future held. I knew that something would have to change in a way that wouldn't suit Miguel. Either he had to stop seeing Monica or I would have to leave him—I became more afraid of him and more afraid of leaving him. I would check his phone each morning when he was in the shower before work and see that he had talked to Monica for at least half an hour or so the day before. When I returned from a Thanksgiving trip home to New York, the calls were three or more hours long. When I checked the phone the morning after that, it was locked. It was shortly after that when he announced one evening that he had to go into work for a few hours, but when he left he was wearing Timberland cargo sweats and a black t-shirt, not his security guard uniform. While he was gone, I cleaned and disinfected the bathroom, cleaned the floors, picked up the living room, and was washing the dishes when he returned. He walked straight past me and into the shower. I had read enough books and seen enough television programs to know what that meant.

The fighting, which had subsided temporarily, intensified. He was twice my size and was all muscle. He would yell and threaten to damage my belongings or my car or me. He hit things. An angry man, he was an ex-Marine, and there were weapons in the apartment. And so I hid. I would hide from him anywhere I could find. I hid under the dining room table or behind the headboard between the bed and the wall or in the cupboards or behind a rack of clothes in the closet. He'd search the apartment for me, screaming, threatening, and punching walls and doors. So I hid.

(Photo courtesy of Bill Thompson)

25

Seattle

<hr />

About 154,000 veterans across the country. . . .
are homeless on any given night; and up to twice as
many experience homelessness at some point during
the course of a year. Veterans represent over 25 per-
cent of the total homeless population; most are male.
However, the VA recently reported that the number
of women veterans has grown from three percent a
decade ago to five percent. The share of younger
homeless women veterans is almost double—
nine percent of homeless veterans are under age 45.
In addition, women veterans are four times more
likely than their civilian counterparts to become
homeless (in comparison, male veterans are 1.25
times more likely to be homeless than their civilian
counterparts).

From: "California's Women Veterans: Challenges and Needs,"
by Lisa Foster, California Research Bureau, March 29, 2010

One night I told Miguel I was taking Grizzly for a walk. I put the puppy on his leash and took him down to the parking lot. Miguel monitored everything I did, including who I talked to, what I wore, where I went—even exactly where I took Grizzly on his walks. I knew I could not leave the parking lot, so walking the dog meant standing with him a few feet from the building. If Miguel checked and saw that I wasn't nearby, he would grill me about where I had been and accuse me of meeting up with someone or other, and then there'd be another huge argument.

As Grizzly and I stood on the grassy margin that ran along the back edge of the parking lot, I turned my back to the building, removed my phone from my pocket, and, without looking at it, dialed the number of a friend in Seattle. Leslie had served in Iraq with me, was assigned to Camp TQ, and worked with us in Mortuary Affairs whenever our work load became impossible to keep up with. He was just about the only volunteer who stuck it out and who didn't leave after helping with just a few bodies. If Miguel wasn't the Marine I had thought he was, Leslie would be. He would have given his life for me in Iraq, and I would have given mine for him. I knew that Leslie, who had left the Marines and was working for a shipping services company, would come to St. Louis to rescue me, would take me back to Seattle, and would provide protection while I got back on my feet and started up a new life.

The phone rang. I held it against my right ear, the one away from the apartment building and Miguel's sightline and held my right arm close to my body, keeping it from jutting out and revealing my secret. Leslie picked up. I had all I could do to not bawl. I explained that I was being abused and was trapped, that I needed a friend to help me pack my things, and a place to stay for a short time while I found my way. I said that there was no one else I could turn to. Because I was never sure if Miguel was secretly watching me from behind, I occasionally swiveled my head slightly from one side to another while I talked to Leslie. I tilted it upward as though I were staring at a star, or downward, toward the dog, trying to make it appear like I wasn't carrying on a conversation. I explained that it had to be Leslie who came for me because Leslie was a Marine and Miguel wouldn't beat a female in front of another male Marine, what with the Marine code and all. He would not dishonor the Corps so blatantly. But Leslie wanted no part of the mess I was in. Through tears, I told him that I was at my wit's end, that I couldn't take this life any longer, and I begged him to fly to St. Louis to escort me out of this terrible existence. He refused.

Two days later, when Miguel and I were leaving for work, suddenly, without warning, he was enraged: he punched a picture of us that I had framed and hung on the wall by the door. I had no idea what brought this on. Maybe my slacks were too tight or my shampoo too scented, or maybe he would have preferred something other than whatever I had made him for lunch that day. The glass shattered into a thousand shards and blood dripped from Miguel's hand. I called work, said I'd be late because of a car that wouldn't start, removed the glass from his hand, then washed, disinfected, and bandaged it. All the while I was wondering how I could escape.

A week later, when we were heading off to work again, I made it look as though I were a bit behind schedule, so Miguel left the apartment first. Twenty minutes later my mom and her husband pulled into the parking lot in their Ford 250 pickup, hauling a huge racing car trailer. We packed most of my belongings in the trailer and the rest in the back of my Volkswagen bug. They turned around and headed back to New York and I sped toward Seattle, where I knew Miguel would never find me.

Leslie had refused to come to St. Louis, but he was a squared away Marine, and Marines take care of each other. We are trained to put the other first, at all costs. We are trustworthy and loyal and we protect our own. We don't lie and we don't cheat. Miguel had a problem with living according to the Marine code, and Leslie had a momentary lapse when he refused to come to my aid, but I continued to believe completely in that way of life and in my fellow Marines. Plus, Leslie and I had served together. He was, in a way, a member of my platoon. We were closer than brothers, or closer than a brother and sister. Moving to Seattle would bring me back to that world of deep camaraderie and meaning, but this time I'd get to enjoy it in a safe haven, far from Iraq. I was ready to get my old—yet new-and-improved—life underway.

It's a long drive from St. Louis to Seattle. Somewhere in Montana, when the relief of having escaped unharmed and the euphoria of finally getting my life back began to subside, I became aware of my mind trying to make sense of the chaos that my life had become. It was as though I had suddenly realized that the back window was cracked and the wind was whistling through it. I'd be gazing at an unfamiliar landscape or shutting off my directional signal after coming back into line from the passing lane when I'd catch my brain, on its own, without my conscious help, trying to explain how it was that I was here, on this highway, alone. *When and why had my life gone so wrong? Did my parents and teachers set me up to fail by having me believe that I could do anything, be anyone? Maybe I should have listened to the coach of my Little League team who was trying to tell me that the opposite was true when he refused to play me that summer long ago. Maybe he was right, maybe his lesson was the more honest and humane: "Understand this, little girl. It's really cute that you're wearing a uniform like the boys have on, but there are limits. There are limits inside you and there are limits outside of you, built into this team and its coaches, built into this league and its traditions, and built into this society and its history. Play around with all of this if you wish, sweetie, but beware!"*

My brain wouldn't stop.

Or was it the Marines who set me up to fail, who put me on this highway to who knows where? I believed in the Corps and all of the virtues it embodied. I wanted to be honest and true and brave. I wanted to sacrifice for others and for what was right, and if I could earn some respect for having done so, wonderful. But maybe I should have given more thought to the recruiter's comment when he said, "Females aren't allowed to be on a tank crew." That, after all, isn't just

idle chit-chat or a superfluous, throwaway line. It symbolically repre-
sents the limits of history and tradition, attitudes and beliefs, a division
of labor and a hierarchy that soon enough would have me standing
behind *my platoon or, bloodied and beaten by a man more than twice*
my size, standing, bowed, *with my hands on my knees, in front of*
scores of male Marines who sit there being entertained, and feeling
satisfied that the Corps is still the Corps, and, no matter what, will
always be the Corps.

Maybe I was conned too by television stations with their reruns of
happy wives in loving relationships in stable families. Since leaving
Iraq, I tried to be that woman. I was feminine and made-up and had
my nails done. I spent my free time cooking and baking and cleaning.
I even bought the most feminine car I could find on eBay, a blue
Volkswagen beetle. I was accommodating and deferential and down-
right sweet and . . . for what? To be lied to and humiliated and pushed
around? Maybe, instead of just being hurt and angry when my parents
divorced, I should have seen in the dissolution the wide gap between the
ideal and the real. I should have somehow come to the realization that
the latter—the "real"—has limitations built into it that are largely
beyond my control. Maybe you're the nicest person in the world and are
married to or living with the second nicest person in the world, but that
relationship is made up of understandings and expectations and beliefs
and values that you must abide by, and maybe they're not fair or they're
not suited to your temperament or we've become too self-interested to
bother abiding by them. Or maybe the other doesn't abide by them, in
which case you're also pretty much fucked, and alone, on US-212, in
Montana.

I listened in as it occurred to my brain that every established way of
interacting with one another is based upon a hidden lie that makes
you believe one thing when, in fact, beneath the surface, there's
something very different going on. *Do this and you'll find meaning*
or happiness or glory or lasting love! That's what we're told. In fact,
we're sort of told that we *must* do it if we are to reach our goal. And

so we do it. All of our social groupings, from the Little League to our families, are built on this major deception. All of them . . . *except for a deployed platoon in a war zone.* That is real. You depend upon each other, need each other, sacrifice for each other, and love each other. For real. There's nothing phony about it. It may be because you *must* if you are to survive, and it may be that you tell yourself that you do all of this not for yourself, but only for the other, but it is still real.

I really didn't want to think about any of this, and, besides, it's not at all my habit to blame anyone or anything for the choices I make. No way was it my parents' or the Corps' fault. Nor was it some hidden deceit undergirding arrangements like marriage or a cohabiting boyfriend-girlfriend relationship that's at fault here. I messed up my own life. And now I would straighten it out.

I really did not want to process any of this, but the road was long and I was alone and, sometimes, and increasingly, my brain had a mind of its own. It tried to make sense of what was missing, like it did when we were in the convoy driving through Iraqi villages that were decimated and abandoned. *Where are the people? Where is the movement? Where are the doors from those houses?* My brain was doing the same now. *Where are my friends? My Marines? My family? Why isn't there someone here with me, now? Or waiting for me?*

Once in Seattle, I was offered a tiny, windowless, basement storage room in Leslie's mom's house. It was filled with clothes, books, videos, knickknacks, exercise equipment, and a hundred other artifacts of family life from a decade earlier. A narrow three-foot walkway was carved through the clutter, from the door to the bed. The morning after arriving, I applied for jobs at every sandwich shop, coffee house, and retail store I could find. I posted my resume listing my service as my only qualification on monster.com. I was offered nothing.

Three days into my stay I felt shaky when I discovered my brain thinking again without my permission. *What if the bonds that the*

Corps creates can be sustained only in the Corps? What if Miguel's un-Marine-like behavior was not an aberration? What if the dishonesty, disloyalty, and selfishness of the civilian world return once we leave the Corps? What if Leslie's refusal to come to St. Louis to help me was not a lapse in judgment but was the typical behavior of an ex-Marine?

I reluctantly allowed myself to think this possibility through. It did seem to me that the MA Marines who reenlisted were doing better than those who had left. I occasionally heard reports about one or another of us getting seriously messed up, but it was always after we EASed. Then there were those who left, found civilian life unbearable, then reenlisted. Maybe my brain was right. If it were, what would this mean for me? Should I re-enlist? I couldn't bear the thought of again participating in the kinds of things I once did. Could I become a civilian contractor in Iraq? Would that give me the social grounding I sought but with a way out if I were told to do something I thought was wrong? Or should I have just stayed with Miguel? If he's the closest I can get to the meaningful ties I experienced in Iraq, maybe that will have to do, even if it was only meaning's memory he now embodied. Besides, in several ways he treated me like the Corps did when he controlled and belittled and intimidated me, while receiving my love and admiration. Five days after arriving in Seattle, I was back in the beetle, headed to Tucson, where Miguel had gone when I left St. Louis.

(Photo courtesy of Bill Thompson)

26

A Break

Anger is usually a central feature of a survivor's response to trauma because it is a core component of the survival response in humans. Anger helps people cope with life's adversities by providing us with increased energy to persist in the face of obstacles. However, uncontrolled anger can lead to a continued sense of being out of control of oneself and can create multiple problems in the personal lives of those who suffer from PTSD.

From: "Why is Anger a Common Response to Trauma?"
—National Center for PTSD, Updated October 2003

Somewhere close to Elko, Nevada, I pulled into a McDonalds for a cup of hot chocolate and a break from driving. Close by sat an obese woman and two overweight children who appeared to be hers. The mother was still eating when her kids got up from the table and began playing a variation of the game "tag." They were unable to actually run, but they tried their best, waddling excitedly, swaying a bit as they followed each other around the dining room, eventually administering a tap, then heading off in the opposite direction. Within a couple of minutes, they began squealing when a tag was forthcoming, and emitting a yelp when one was made. One would try to elude the chaser by squeezing into the empty seat of an otherwise occupied booth, only to be cornered and, by then, poked. This continued for ten minutes while the mother maintained a studied focus on the food before her. The rest of us were unable to concentrate on or think about anything except for the commotion that was unfolding. Or the possibility of locking the woman in a choke hold and putting her to sleep. But her neck was so thick and her mouth and esophagus so blocked with that steady stream of slightly masticated food, that I was afraid I'd kill her. Finally, an elderly woman pushed herself up from a table some ten or so feet away, walked over to the mother, and wagged a finger in her face, saying, "You should be ashamed of yourself. You are a horrible mother."

Instead of asking for an explanation or apologizing, the woman, with her mouth still full, extended her arms outward while clinging to what looked like the last bite of a Big Mac, bounced in her seat slightly, and shouted, "You don't know me! Who the fuck are you to tell me I'm a horrible mother? You don't know how I raise my kids, you old bag!"

The mother decided she could do—or refrain from doing— whatever she wanted, believing that her behavior had no effect on anyone else. *Typical. Consume everything in sight while your kids run amok, disrupting other people's lives. Then go ballistic when someone complains, as if it's you who should be angry.* I thought it'd be cool to instantly transport her to Iraq, insert her into a platoon and, after five minutes or so, ask her what she thought then about her interconnectedness with others. Her self-centeredness would be such a huge life and death concern to everyone else that they'd knock it out of her immediately. She was still shouting as I left. By the time I pulled back onto the highway, my brain was in overdrive.

So that's what happens. The solidarity that makes life bearable and the sacrifice that makes love true no longer find fertile soil in American culture—except within the Marine Corps and then maybe only during a deployment in time of war. And once one has experienced that love, they know what they are missing when it's gone. If they reenlist and fight again, they're fine. If they reenlist but do not see combat, they may still experience that bonding at a sufficient enough depth to be okay. If they instead cling desperately to other ex-Marines in the belief that they can, on their own, each give more than they take, they are in trouble. The structural supports a society needs to sustain friendships over individual interests, or the institutions of marriage and family over individual interests, or the neighborhood or the future generation over individual interests, simply do not exist.

Hours and miles passed when I decided to take another break. I might have been in Arizona or maybe I was still in Nevada when I entered an Applebee's, sat at the bar, and ordered a drink. I didn't really have to use the restroom—I had learned to hold it in for days if I had to—but I went anyway. I wasn't hungry, so I didn't eat. My plan was to rest for a few minutes, long enough to stop the feel of the road rolling by beneath me. At a table across from the bar sat a couple in their mid-twenties, each playing intently with a phone, neither paying any attention to the other. When the waitress appeared, the man lifted his eyes to her for a moment, nodded, and returned to the plastic rectangle. The woman never looked up from hers. I was wondering how long this would go on when a television voice mentioned Iraq. I glanced up at the screen above the bar. Usually when this occurred I'd walk away from the television until I could no longer make out what was being said. This time I watched. The story was about a controversy regarding the "flag-draped coffins" that were returning to America from Iraq. Should the public be allowed to view photographs of the coffins or not? This, apparently, was a big issue. One guest argued that, of course, Americans should be shown the coffins. Otherwise, he said, they'll have no idea of what is going on in our war over there. The second expert disagreed vehemently. He asserted that our citizens know perfectly well what's going on in Iraq and displaying the photos would only hurt the families of the dead. Their disagreement became heated.

I felt sick as I remembered why I don't listen to "news" stories about the war. Like the rest of the civilian population, the pundits didn't have a clue as to what they were talking about. But they were supposed to know! It was their job to help inform and educate the public about important issues like war! From a photograph of flag-draped coffins Americans would somehow know what was going on in Iraq? Or they already knew what was happening over there? *Really?* The anger again welled up in my chest. Had I wanted to, I could easily have taken out all of the idiots who participated in the production of this nonsense. That's what I was trained to do. Instead of plotting a strategy to do just that, I hit the road.

I was on US-93, two hours south of the Applebee's, when I felt something break. At first I thought it was one of my ribs—given that they were basically exposed and, depending on what I was wearing, visible even through my blouse. For a moment I thought that maybe the muscle strain I had experienced when moving my belongings into the trailer in St. Louis was something more severe. Maybe I had broken a rib. But after running a hand down one side of my rib cage and up the other, I realized it was something else that had broken, but I didn't know what.

27

Tucson

Survivors with PTSD often think that the world is a very dangerous place. You may think it is likely that you will be harmed again. If you have PTSD, living in a high-crime area may confirm these beliefs and make you more fearful. If it is possible, move to a safer area. It may then be easier for you to rethink your beliefs about danger. You may be better able to trust that you will be safe.

From: "Lifestyle Changes Recommended for PTSD Patients," United States Department of Veterans Affairs, January 1, 2007

Miguel and I ended up together again in a very small one-bedroom, ground-floor apartment on Tucson's south side. To me, it could have been Mexico. Everyone spoke Spanish, many of the road signs were in Spanish, and every job required that one speak Spanish. I didn't speak Spanish. As it turned out, that wasn't that big a deal because I never left the apartment.

By this point in time, I was experiencing symptoms of a social phobia. I simply could not leave the apartment—the apartment I hated being in. My incentive to go outside was lessened by the very high crime rate that characterized the neighborhood. Day in and day out I remained inside with the blinds closed and the door locked. I couldn't go to the grocery store or the library or the doctor's office. As the landlord no longer allowed pets, I no longer had Grizzly's company. I was imprisoned . . . alone . . . except for—and this was when the rumination began—my memories of and my thoughts about Iraq. Until now Iraq had just been a part of my job as a Marine. It was what I had trained for and what I did. But images and doubts that I hadn't before entertained fully began creeping into my consciousness. Alone, in that tiny apartment, I began questioning what we were doing in Iraq and what *I* had done there. Initially, I struggled with issues related to the Corps' standard operating procedures and my own adherence to them, but before long I was tormented by basic philosophical and, especially, moral questions. Why had we invaded another country? How could I have been complicit in a war that hurt so many innocent people? I tried to see the honor in what I had done over there, but couldn't. I searched for meaning in the deaths of the soldiers and civilians I helped to bury, but I could not find it. I had put my faith in the Marine Corps, believing that they knew more than me, knew better than me, and now I was losing that faith.

I started to drink.

I became convinced that others could tell that I had served in Iraq and what it was, exactly, that I had done there. It felt as though the stigma that had marked me as a deviant at Camp TQ had followed me here. This conviction provided another reason to not leave the apartment. To hide the past from myself, I packed away all signs of my military service: my cammies and uniforms, boots and covers. I didn't keep a single EGA pin or boot band. I buried my medals and ribbons deep in the back of our small closet because they upset me the most. I'd think about what it was I did to earn them and the shame would wash over me. To hide the past from myself, I dressed in as feminine a way as I could: tight clothes— with lace and flowers—that fit the form of my body, and high heels. My hair was done and my eyebrows waxed.

Nothing worked. I hid from those who might have guessed I had been a Marine, and I hid from the artifacts of my service, and I hid from the toughened veteran deep inside me by covering her up with a cloak of femininity, and I hid from it all by drinking, but I could still not mute the memories or quiet the doubts.

One early evening I sat in the dark apartment watching a local television show when I was startled by a loud banging on the door. *Bang! Bang! Bang!* I didn't answer the door because I didn't know a soul in the neighborhood given that I never left the apartment. Plus, it wasn't as though an elderly neighbor were gently knocking on the door—the door was being pounded. Nor was it Miguel, who, of course, had a key and who, if he misplaced the key, would call or text. Someone I did not know was punching the door hard with the side of a fist. *Bang! Bang! Bang!* I could hear several voices speaking rapidly in Spanish. I sat motionless, nervous, hoping they would eventually go away. I held my breath. Maybe they were gone. *Bang! Bang! Bang!* This time the knocking didn't stop but increased in rate and intensity. *Do they think the apartment is empty and are planning to steal what they can? Or do they know I'm in here?* I picked up the cell phone by my side and called Miguel who was at work. He told me to get the gun that was on the top shelf of the bedroom closet. But doing so would risk being seen by the intruders through the cracks around the shade covering the window adjacent to the door. Miguel could barely hear my whisper above the relentless pounding. *Bang! Bang! Bang! Bang! Bang!* He told me he'd be home right away. I wasn't moving because I didn't want them to see me, and because I was frozen with fear. *Bang! Bang! Bang!* The door jam split open. I wondered what was the worst thing they could do to me and thought I had already been through worse than that. *I hate my life, anyway,* I thought. At the moment I was certain the door would spring wide open, I heard Miguel yelling at the would-be intruders from some distance down the block. He ran to the door, armed and wearing his security guard uniform from work. He shouted at them in Spanish and asked what they were doing. They claimed that I had left on my car's headlamps, and they were trying to alert me so the battery wouldn't die. Then the four of them walked away. Miguel checked and found the head lights were on, and then he went back to work. I sat down in front of the television, a few feet from the broken door frame, in the darkened apartment, with the gun by my side.

After months of trying, I convinced Miguel to attend couples' counseling with me at the VA hospital. He never expressed any doubts about the war or his role in it, and he didn't believe that I had a right to do so given that I was not a part of the "real" war, the invasion phase. So his heart was not in this counseling plan of mine. I had reminded him four or five times about our initial appointment, but he didn't show up. When he didn't show up to our second scheduled meeting, the counselor told me that he wouldn't be able to see me anymore as he specialized in couples' counseling. He added that it was clear that I had my own issues to work on and he strongly advised that I set up an appointment for individual counseling.

And so I somehow brought myself to the VA hospital where a group meeting was scheduled for veterans with Post-Traumatic Stress Syndrome. I was the only female in the crowded room. I purposefully dressed in a professional and feminine manner. I'm not sure who the waiting men thought I was, but several of them, one after another, approached me, sat down, and opened up about their troubles, about the unrelenting nightmares and angry outbursts and uncontrollable crying jags. They may have initially guessed that I worked in the facility in some sort of counseling capacity, but after learning that I was a Marine who had spent time I Iraq, they seemed surprised and relieved. *"Don't tell me you were a fucking Marine,"* they would say with anticipation. After which I would respond with a muted, half-hearted Marine bark: *hoorah.* It was then that they started to talk about their experiences. After an hour or so my name was called and I was asked to meet separately with a counselor. The second her office door closed behind me I burst into tears. I could not stop crying. I was unable to speak. I cried and cried. I cried for thirty minutes, until the appointment came to a close. I did not say a single word but I left with prescriptions for an antidepressant, anti-anxiety medication, and a sleep aid.

Each week I'd see a psychiatrist and a counselor. The former had to be in his late seventies. He didn't seem interested in hearing about my problems. It was as though he had heard them all already. He was there to sign the prescription pad, which he seemed to do automatically. The counselor tried to help me with my all-consuming guilt and depression, but she herself wasn't military and the distance between us yawned widely. How could she possibly understand what I was dealing with? She didn't know how young, healthy men could disappear into thin air in an instant, leaving behind a boot or finger or head. She had never amassed remains that were unidentifiable as having once belonged to a human being, let alone a specific individual. She never experienced the guilt associated with having succumbed to the pressure to pose near a sign that reads, "Napalm sticks to kids," or to assist in the degradation of a proud young Marine who is four pounds heavier than regulations allow. She may have a hint of what it feels like to have every aspect of your physical being critically assessed by nearby men, but she can't understand fully what it's like when the assessments are crude and explicit and unending and the men are a horde and you are alone. She cannot possibly empathize with a twenty-year-old girl who learns her colleague, himself a husband and father, had to hand an Iraqi man two bags containing the remains of his wife and four year old daughter. The counselor tried her best to help me but she could not. I attempted to find the words that would help her to understand what I had been through and what I was going through, but I could not. I just could not find the words. My social anxiety had become so overwhelming that at the end of our session—and each subsequent session—the counselor had to walk me out to my car.

Soon it became too difficult to get *to* the appointments. I couldn't leave the apartment. I was too afraid that others would see me for who I was: a completely fucked-up human being who had gone to Iraq and done unspeakable things and who was now doing nothing whatsoever except contributing to a horrible, horrible relationship. I continued to take the medications without the counseling. The sleep aid they gave me transformed me into a potato. I would take it half an hour before going to bed and it would shut off my brain. I was able to sit on the couch and stare at the television with nothing whatsoever in my head. The circuitry had shut down and I was free-floating in a spaced-out zone where there was nothing to worry about because there was nothing at all. During this thirty minute interval, I could be sure that my brain wouldn't start thinking on its own, without my cooperation. I enjoyed this feeling, so I took the pill every night.

Until, that is, Miguel caught me getting my medications from where I hid them in a shoebox in the back of the closet. He started yelling and threw the pills to the floor. He reminded me that I was never a *real* Marine, that I was too weak to be a *real* Marine, so weak that I had to rely upon fucking drugs. The drugs were only making me more fucked up, he shouted. That was the night I stopped taking the medications.

28

Nightmare

When Jonathan Schulze came home from Iraq, he tried to live a normal life. But the war kept that from happening.

At first, Jonathan Schulze tried to live with the nightmares and the grief he brought home from Iraq. He was a tough kid from central Minnesota, and more than that, a U.S. Marine to the core.

Yet his moods when he returned home told another story. He sobbed on his parents' couch as he told them how fellow Marines had died, and how he, a machine gunner, had killed the enemy. In his sleep, he screamed the names of dead comrades. He had visited a psychiatrist at the VA hospital in Minneapolis.

Two weeks ago, Schulze went to the VA hospital in St. Cloud. He told a staff member he was thinking of killing himself, and asked to be admitted to the mental health unit, said his father and stepmother, who accompanied him. They said he was told he couldn't be admitted that day. The next day, as he spoke to a counselor in St. Cloud by phone, he was told he was No. 26 on the waiting list, his parents said.

Four days later, Schulze, 25, committed suicide in his New Prague home.

From: "This Marine's Death Came After He Served in Iraq,"
by Kevin Giles, *The Star Tribune*, January 27, 2007

After convincing Miguel that I'd never find a decent job without going to college and that going to college in New York would be cheaper than it would be in Arizona, he did not object when I packed up the beetle once more and headed east. I knew we couldn't live together and he did too, and I wasn't at all sure that I could live alone. So the break wasn't a clean one. We would talk and text every day and I would come back when time allowed.

The first two months home I spent on my father's sofa. Both the television and my thoughts ran continuously but I tried to not pay attention to either. Worried, my dad convinced me to visit the youth pastor at the Bemus Point Methodist church to share with him what had happened to my life since I was sixteen. He immediately got me involved in church activities, such as working with toddlers and babysitting in the nursery, but I couldn't shake my lethargy or find any motivation, and two weeks later was back on the couch. It became increasingly difficult for me to sleep and, when I did sleep, I had nightmares.

I am in the desert, surrounded by the flat beige of an endless expanse of sand. We are under attack. In front of us, extending for miles is the thick four-foot tall protective berm we hastily erected out of sand and sand bags. There is gear and equipment scattered around us—quadcons (large bulletproof storage containers), 40-foot storage containers, discarded canteens and LBVs (plate armor vests worn to absorb the impact of bullets). Our berm absorbs the bulk of enemy ground fire but we are assaulted from the air as well. I keep my head down, following my platoon and running along the length of the berm through the tedious sugar sand. I can hear the roar of small aircraft overhead, dropping bombs all around us. Mortar shells whistle over our heads from across the berm. The combination of explosions and the sandy wind mutes the sound of my comrades shouting to one another. I am running as fast as I can manage with the heavy burden of my equipment, trying to keep up with my platoon. I pause for a moment to lay down protective fire over the top of the berm, but when I take aim and squeeze the trigger of my M-16 nothing happens. Thinking that the weapon has jammed, I eject the magazine and am panicked to realize that I have no ammunition. I resume running, and rummage frantically through my belongings for any spare rounds. Finding nothing, I begin searching the discarded gear on the ground as I continue the slog through the sand. I scan the bodies of wounded and fallen Marines, their limbs broken and turned at awkward angles, looking for any magazines or ammunition that I can scavenge and use.

I would jolt awake, sweating, terrified.

My father finally let me know that he wasn't going to enable me forever. He would not stand by and provide the wherewithal that allowed me to stay on that couch. It was hard for him, but he made it clear that I had to stand up, on my own two feet, and, if not make something *of* myself, at least make a life *for* myself. I put my gear in my car and drove one town over, to my mother's house, where I parked myself on her couch.

I awaken still groggy from sleep at "zero dark-thirty" (before sun-up) in my barracks room. The room is constructed from cement block walls covered in chipped and faded beige paint. The floor is covered with cold tan tiles. I know that I have to be suited up in cammies at formation soon so I begin gathering the pieces of my uniform. I retrieve my tee-shirt, black socks, trousers, belt, cover, and blouse from my locker and pile them on my rack. Upon inspecting my blouse however, I notice that my chevrons (rank insignia worn on the collar) are missing. "Oh shit! You've got to be kidding me" I think, frustrated that this easily lost or damaged component of my uniform is not in its proper place. I begin rifling through the top shelf of my locker, realizing with increasing anxiety that I don't have time to go to the PX (Marine Corps Convenience Store) to buy new chevrons. I sift through the items in my locker, such as extra boot laces, boot polish kit and extra belt, but can't see any trace of the missing chevrons. Frustrated, I check my blouse once more and then scan the room frantically, knowing that I have to come up with some kind of plan to avoid the inevitable ass-chewing I'll be treated to by the squad leader and platoon sergeant. I consider going to formation without my chevrons, but I know that this would mean spending the day as a private, doing the dirtiest work on base all day, risking reprimand and even a "page 11" (written citation in my permanent service record). Then I notice that something else is amiss in the room. I see a strange shape in the corner. Crumpled in the shadows is my room-mate. I move closer to investigate and realize that she is dead. I feel a sense of relief, as I know that she is the same rank as me. I check her collar and find the chevrons I need and pin them on my blouse. The crisis averted, I leave the room and head for formation.

I was slipping further away from the person I once was and the woman I thought I'd become, and I did not know what to do about it. I enrolled at the nearby community college, in part because it meant I could live in the vacant apartment over my father's downtown office, where I would have my own couch to live on, free from the judgments of my parents. As an added benefit, I'd get to run up and down the stairs four or five times whenever I left the apartment. My short-term memory loss, which helped me psychologically at Camp TQ, aided me aerobically now as I'd realize only when getting to my car that I forgot the keys, and then, once in the car, that I forgot my phone, and then a book I had planned to return to the library, and so on.

Living alone I began to really focus on what my brain had been trying to figure out since at least St. Louis. *Why were we fighting this war? Why had I volunteered? What is the allure of the Marines? Is there anyone who understands anything about the widespread suffering that is going on? Forget about the flag draped coffins themselves, is there anyone who knows what's in them and what those remains tell us about the nature of that war or, for that matter, the nature of life and death?*

My depression flourished and sleeping became almost impossible. I would come home after school and just sit on my couch or lay on my bed staring at the walls or the ceiling, wrestling with these questions. Night after night was the same. I started drinking again to help me sleep, but after a short time I was drinking too much. So I'd sit there, drunk, listening to Tom Waits on repeat singing or talking or doing whatever it is he does through a voice box containing the sand-encrusted gears of an MEP 803 generator instead of the usual cartilage, membrane, and tissue, to let us know that a character is wasted and wounded, on his knees, begging to be stabbed in the chest. I'd consciously wish I were the guy in that song, and more than anything else, I wanted the dagger to be buried. I'd call up YouTube on my laptop and play again and again and again Drowning Pool's *Let the Bodies Hit the Floor*—the United States Marine Corps' version. Flashbacks would start up and I'd suddenly find myself in Iraq, processing an endless line of bodies that were no longer recognizable as such. I'd get wasted and eventually throw up. Often I passed out on the bathroom floor, or I'd make it only as far as the kitchen, and pass out there. On a good night I'd make it to the bedroom, if not into the bed itself. I would wake up not knowing where I was. Too scared to move, I would only very slowly and carefully open my eyes, just a crack, to see if I could recognize something in the environment that would give a hint as to where I was. Even with my eyes wide open I wasn't always sure where I was or how I got there.

I fought to focus on my coursework and spent hours every day studying, which left less and less time for drinking and ruminating. I wanted to excel academically, to get an A in every course I took, but I also wanted to figure out what had happened to me. The latter did not come easily and I still do not understand it all fully. Often, the most enlightening and helpful pieces of knowledge I acquired were also the most painful to grapple with. Each time I made a bit of progress intellectually, and then psychologically and physically, I would soon after slip up. I'd learn something about the nature of war that increased my awareness of what I had experienced, but that awareness itself would become an added burden, and so I would drink. I would grasp an insight into the structure of our society or the content of our culture that would clarify what I had not before seen clearly, but the light would be too harsh, and I would retreat into my apartment and not leave for days. I learned about resilience and selflessness, but the hope that knowledge offered highlighted the gap between where I could one day be and where I was, and that chasm, in the bright light, was so wide that it became even more difficult for me to eat; so I—at 5' 9" and not much more than 100 pounds—would read about the power of human resilience while sipping the dietary supplement Ensure. Although I was withering away, I fought to understand and to believe in the capacity of the mind and body to return to its original state after being twisted beyond recognition. After a night of studying, when I would integrate my new knowledge into my old experiences, I'd feel stronger. Until I fell to sleep.

It is mid-day in a dense Jungle. The bright light filters through the leaves and is dim by the time it reaches the ground. I can sense the approaching threat of enemies who are pursuing us. My platoon and I attempt to escape. We spot some vines hanging from the tops of the massive towering trees and form a desperate plan to evade our pursuers. We rush to the vines and immediately begin climbing upwards. The vines, which are thick and knotted, are overhanging a wide, green, deep river. The river is so deep and dark that we can't even see into the water. In the background I am surrounded only by a blur of various shades of black and green. Soon we realize with terror that the enemy is approaching us in canoes on the river. As they open fire on us with various weapons such as AK's and harpoons, we struggle to climb but are afforded little cover, as we are hanging in mid-air over the river. Some members of the platoon are able to climb more easily, but others like me struggle to overcome the weight of our equipment. I become more frustrated as my gear becomes tangled in the vines.

When the drinking became too much work, I started smoking weed, which suppressed the pain better than the booze had. And so

I smoked all the time. I smoked to get out of bed and to eat and to leave the apartment and to sleep and to get up again the next morning. An eighth of an ounce a week became a quarter of an ounce and soon a quarter ounce lasted only a couple of days. I was numbed enough to . . . to persist . . . to continue . . . breathing, but the drug would wear off and I would ruminate and then, with restless sleep, the nightmares returned.

This is me standing in front of the clock tower in Chautauqua Institution in NY. It stands on the edge of the lake where I grew up. (Author collection)

29

Chautauqua

Only the educated are free.

—Epictetus

On the northwest shore of Chautauqua Lake sits the Chautauqua Institution, an adult education center founded in the late 1800s. Originally a destination where men and women could engage in self-directed studies that would lead to intellectual and moral improvement, it became a national venue where political leaders and ordinary citizens could discuss issues of domestic and international importance. Perhaps it was its emphasis on self-improvement or life-long learning or its promotion of open political discussion that prompted President Theodore Roosevelt to proclaim that Chautauqua was the most American thing in America. It seemed fitting, then, that it was here, on Chautauqua Lake, where I had grown up, that I found myself seeking knowledge and moral grounding in and outside of the college classroom.

I read about war. It wasn't easy to do, especially when authors didn't know what they were talking about. It was also difficult when they did. One excellent book that helped me to understand all that I had been through is Chris Hedges' *War Is A Force That Gives Us Meaning.* I hadn't a clue that *all* wars are based upon lies and myths; nor had I understood that because the warrior knows the lies, first hand, a tension develops between him or her and the power elite that fabricates them. The warrior also experiences tension with the ordinary citizens who spread the lies and who, by the way, would rather not know the truth. Until reading this book, I thought that I alone carried the burden of a terrible secret, one that, once shared—if it dared be—would change the course of the war and the fortunes of our leaders. I also didn't know that far from an isolated aberration, it is the virtually unwavering tendency of the press to perpetuate those myths by glorifying the savagery of war.

I read about the nature of society in general. An essay by Peter Berger helped me to see that all ongoing social arrangements, not just war, are based upon a lie, an element of deception that allows so many of us, at the same time and place, to pattern our interactions and to form the social groupings that are essential to orderliness and meaning. Marriages hold us together, for example, in part only to the extent that we believe they are not just the best but the *only* way to experience sustained love. Wars are fought, in part, because we believe that they are the *only* way to resolve extraordinary international political problems. Without myths, the patterned relationships that allow us to share a life will break down, and each of us, as individuals, may spin off into a state of destructive isolation.

I read C. Wright Mills, including several essays suggesting that truth is not necessarily the enemy of society, or at least not the enemy of the *good* society. It is deception and fabrication that are the adversaries of robust communities within democratic societies. Courageous acts required by war need not be based upon lies. Honest, committed, relationships need not be fostered by myths. Democratic decision-making need not be distorted by the falsehoods of the powerful. Hard work and the dignity it bestows need not be degraded into a form of mindless servitude and then falsely called a "career" as if it were capable of building character or nations. Hope that motivates our behavior and gives us a reason to go on need not be cheapened into fantasy by being rooted in a corporation's marketing strategy. Illusions and lies need not replace reality.

I concluded that there are good myths and bad myths. Myths can be benign. They can emerge organically from shared lives, embody and preserve the ideals of that life, provide a yardstick with which to measure the shortcomings of reality, and, finally, help to bring reality more into line with the shared ideals. Or myths can be malignant. They can be imposed by the powerful to further their interests at the expense of everybody else's. They can supplant reality. They can undermine the true bases of a shared life, leaving each of us on our own, frightened, compliant, craving entertainment, dying to consume. The absence of benign myths may result in an atomization of society. The presence of malignant ones do the same.

I concluded that too many of the myths surrounding war are malignant.

C. Wright Mills also helped me to appreciate the value of linking my biography to the structure and history of society. I could see that only under particular social and historical circumstances are females encouraged to excel academically and physically; or are allowed to enlist in the military, carry weapons, and be deployed to war zones. Only within a definite type of social environment are females subject to incessant harassment without any meaningful recourse. Only in certain times and places will a nation engage in a preemptive war or be able to transport a huge war machine across the globe. This perspective helped me to understand more clearly that when tens of thousands of veterans return home suffering from the same set of symptoms, the issues I am struggling with are not simply an individual problem of mine, with only individual causes and solutions; they are at the same time social in cause and resolution.

I read and majored in psychology and learned that one of its most consistent findings is that, contrary to our common-sensical understandings, selfishness is correlated with *un*happiness. When one considers the interests and feelings of others, and insists upon giving at least as much as she takes, *she* benefits. The work of psychologists Roy Baumeister and Jean Twenge and W. Keith Campbell helped me realize that self-discipline and self-control are undervalued virtues today and that unearned self-esteem and narcissism on the other hand leave their victims anxious and depressed. This is the dark side of unwarranted self-esteem. My reading consistently underscored the benefits of good counseling. From psychology I also became aware of the healing power of resilience as well as the necessity of good friendships, families, and communities to provide sustenance to resilience.

I read philosophy and benefited so much from doing so that I minored in it. I sought answers to questions about morality and God and justice and happiness and forgiveness; I wanted to know what it is that makes a person or a society "good," and what, if anything, comes after death. My journey took me to Socrates,

Plato, Aristotle, Kant, Nietzsche, and St. Thomas Aquinas. When I stopped to rest and reflect, I could discern the commonalties among the best of the social scientists and philosophers, and was able to piece together a worldview of sorts, of which the following is a part.

The close bonds and deep meaning that characterize a Marine platoon can be created in the wider social world, even if not so easily in our own. And, importantly, the conditions that foster closeness and meaning in the Marines needn't be forced upon us. We can choose to be good based upon knowledge and truth, and upon freedom and choice. The traits that make a person "good"— knowledge and wisdom and courage and justice and honesty and humility and an ability to focus on what is important outside of oneself, among others—can be cultivated and used to make relationships and communities "good." A good community in turn will encourage virtues and will promote sacrifice, and sacrifice will generate meaning and love, both of which will be all the sweeter because they are freely chosen. This is what I believe. This is my hope.

This was taken inside the female tent in tent city at Camp TQ. Some of us were active duty Marines, some were Marine reservists, two of us were corpsmen, and one of us was an Army reservist. (Author collection)

30

Hope

---

*What oxygen is to the lungs, such is
hope to the meaning of life.*

—Emil Brunner

After graduating I took some time off from school and briefly stayed with Miguel in Tucson. I soon returned home and enrolled in a four-year institution thirty miles from the community college to continue my education and rehabilitation. I majored in Psychology and minored in Philosophy, started running again and joined the college's concert band. And I continued to encounter setbacks. If, despite my best efforts, a fellow student discovered I had been a Marine and in the war, they would ask what it was I did in Iraq. I could not answer. When they'd ask if I had killed anyone over there, I would not answer. The question was often accompanied by a hint of hopeful expectation that I had indeed taken a life, information they could later share with buddies over beer pong. "Dudes, listen to this: I know a chick who has killed someone!" One day in class a professor mentioned that American Marines are taught to "slaughter" other human beings, not bothering to explain himself and leaving implicit the notion that his assertion was fact, and that the victims were always total innocents, and that those who fought for other nations or groups were taught something different and more humane, and that there is no linguistic or moral distinction between killing and slaughtering, even though every dictionary lists as slaughter's synonyms butcher, murder, and torture.

I struggled to claw my way back to . . . back to *what?* Happiness? No. Normalcy? I didn't think that was any longer possible. Sanity? Maybe. Functionality? Yes, I wanted to be able to function, to sleep and eat and work and, maybe, to one day laugh and love. When I founded a war vets discussion group on campus I sensed I was gaining a small degree of control over my life. When other vets opened up to me I felt the way I did two years earlier, in the waiting room of the VA hospital in Tucson when war-damaged men almost spontaneously disclosed their worst memories and deepest fears to me. In doing so, they made me feel a needed and useful part of a wider community.

When my father and his new wife treated me to dinner the

night before graduation, he asked about my future plans.

"Graduate school," I said. "Psychology. I'd like to become a counselor."

"Psychology? How will you make a living with psychology?"

"I want to try to help out people if I can."

"Become a lawyer. You'll get to help even more people."

"I don't think so."

"That's ninety percent of what a lawyer does—we counsel people, give them advice, help them out of jams. You can join my firm. In fact, I've already come up with a name for it. Goodell and . . ." He paused and glanced upward, as though he were retrieving the remainder of the firm's name from his memory. "Goodell and . . . *Goodell.*"

My progress is unsteady and slow but I experience glimmers of my life, as it was and as I would like it to be. I choose healthy relationships with good people. I try to give to others in a number of ways, including working with children during the summer months, and volunteering at a local food bank and the VA hospital where I am treated. I am also a member of a group of veterans who work to help Iraqi refugees establish new lives in the Boston area, where I now live. In the hospital, with my fellow broken Marines, I revel in a surge of the camaraderie I knew in Iraq. In the apartment of a dislocated Iraqi family, as I sit at their kitchen table eating rice and chicken, I am overwhelmed by a sense of shame.

To the best of my ability I practice the Marine code of honor in my daily life by being honest and hard-working and willing to sacrifice for those who share these fundamental truths. And on the good days, I feel a stirring inside, as the meaning and purpose and closeness and love I once thought dead show signs of life, after all. It is on these days that I am able to lighten the hue of so much I had shaded black. It is then that I am able to hope.

As we were soon to learn, the confusion was in the very ground beneath our feet that would give way like loose sand whenever we tried to propel ourselves forward . . . (Photo courtesy of Bill Thompson)

Epilogue

I saw battle—corpses, myriads of them,
And the white skeletons of young men, I saw them,
I saw the debris and the debris of all the slain
  soldiers of the war,
They themselves were fully at rest, they suffer'd not,
The living remained and suffer'd, the mother
  suffer'd,
And the wife and the child and the musing comrade
  suffer'd,
And the armies that remain'd suffer'd.

—Walt Whitman,
"When Lilacs Last in the Dooryard Bloom'd"

It's been five years since we returned from Iraq. I think about that country, my platoon, and what we did over there often. Daily. During certain stretches of time, continuously. Every now and then I hear from or about one of my Marines. Last month, as I was completing my graduate school application, I received a text from one Mortuary Affairs Marine after he tried unsuccessfully to commit suicide. "I've got $2,000 in the bank," his message read. "Let's meet in NYC and go out with a bang."

The Wound Dresser

But in silence, in dreams' projections,
While the world of gain and appearance and mirth goes on,
So soon what is over forgotten, and waves wash the
      imprints off the sand,
With hinged knees returning I enter the doors, (while for
      you up there,
Whoever you are, follow without noise and be of strong heart.)

Bearing the bandages, water and sponge,
Straight and swift to my wounded I go,
Where they lie on the ground after the battle brought in,
Where their priceless blood reddens the grass the ground,
Or to the rows of the hospital tent, or under the roof'd hospital,
To the long rows of cots up and down each side I return,
To each and all one after another I draw near, not one do I miss,
An attendant follows holding a tray, he carries a refuse pail,
Soon to be fill'd with clotted rags and blood, emptied,
      and fill'd again . . .

Thus in silence in dreams' projections,
Returning, resuming, I thread my way through the hospitals,
The hurt and wounded I pacify with soothing hand,
I sit by the restless all the dark night, some are so young,
Some suffer so much, I recall the experience sweet and sad,
(Many a soldier's loving arms about this neck have cross'd and rested,
Many a soldier's kiss dwells on these bearded lips.)

—Walt Whitman

Afterword

I think of Iraq and my Marines every single day and, still, I cannot understand how we did what we did. The carnage was so pervasive and profound, and most of us were so young. Yet, despite the open option to leave the platoon given us by The Sir, we stayed. Why? We knew we were doing a job that had to be done. We did it for one another, and for our families, and for the Corps. If we were willing to die for each other, we could certainly gather up what remained of each other and send that home.

I also often think about the war itself and the reasons we fought it. Late at night, when I cannot stop the rumination, I try to convince myself that there had to be a purpose that is beyond my knowledge or understanding, and that it is a noble purpose. I pray that we are not killing and being killed for anything as transitory as oil, money, or power. Only then am I able to sleep.

After ending my active service with the Marines, I found myself in a series of situations I did not want to be in. Nothing was right, not the cities, the relationships, the people, or my state of mind. I just didn't belong and could not figure out how to transition myself to a place where I did. Initially, I believed that a good first step would be to bury, somewhere deep inside of me, the memories of my wartime experiences. I tried, but couldn't. I hoped I'd repress that entire period of my life, but that did not happen. Finally, I resolved to accept the doubt and guilt and torment as a burden I would bear. Then John Hearn suggested I do the opposite, that I finally talk about what I had been through. He felt that I could possibly exert greater control over my thoughts if I arranged them into a coherent narrative. He also believed that my story could, in a small way, help others. Our conversation became this book.

Jessica Goodell
March, 2011

Postscript

Jessica Goodell enrolled in one of my courses in the fall of 2006. She appeared a bit older than most of her classmates. She was also very thin. When I picture her in that classroom, it's her posture that I see most clearly. While others had a tendency to slouch down into their plastic chairs or to lean forward to rest their arms on the shared table before them, Jess sat with a perfectly straight spine. She didn't whisper to classmates, play with her phone, or appear disinterested. She finished the course with one of the few "A"s I assigned. I remember too that she did not say a single word throughout the fifteen week semester. She took another course with me in the spring. Again, a straight back, respectful demeanor, excellent work, and not a single word. When she graduated in May of that year, she was named co-recipient of an award that is given annually to the best student in the college's social sciences division.

I didn't see or hear from Jessica again until she appeared at my office door a year or so later. She was on campus and wanted to drop by to say hello. I asked her to sit down and we chatted. She hoped to return to school to become, eventually, a psychologist. Her goal was to one day do research on PTSD and work with its victims. During our conversation she mentioned that she had an "excuse" for being behind schedule educationally. "I was in the military," she said, "the Marines." When our conversation ended, I invited her to visit again when she was next on campus. As she was leaving the office, she paused at the doorway and asked, "Next time, can we talk about forgiveness?"

Jess was dealing with the after effects of both living in a combat zone and working with human remains in a Mortuary Affairs platoon, and they were making her adjustment back into civilian life difficult. The transition was further complicated by the fact that she was leaving a social milieu characterized by self-sacrifice for one that tended to emphasize self-absorption. But there was something else at work too. During a late October afternoon chat, as thick grey clouds gathered outside my office window, it occurred to me that a portion of Jess' trauma stemmed from being female in an environment that was systematically hostile to females. I asked her to imagine herself twenty years down the road, the mother of an eighteen-year-old son.

"What would you tell him if he were to announce that he was enlisting in the Marines?" I asked.

"I'd tell him to go for it," she replied.

"What would you say to an eighteen-year-old daughter who told you she was joining the Marines?"

"I'd say, No you're not."

"No discussion?"

"No."

"No compromising? You wouldn't suggest, for example, that she graduate from college first and then decide whether or not to sign up?"

"No."

"Just a straight-out 'No you're not'?"

"Correct."

John Hearn
March, 2011

Further Reading

Baumeister, Roy F., Laura Smart, and Joseph M. Boden. "Relation of Threatened Egotism to Violence and Aggression: The Dark Side of High Self-esteem." *Psychological Review* 103.1 (1996): 5-33.

Berger, Peter L. *Invitation to Sociology; a Humanistic Perspective.* Woodstock, NY: Overlook Press, 1973.

Hedges, Chris. *War Is a Force That Gives Us Meaning.* New York: Anchor Books, 2003.

Hemingway, Ernest. *"Notes on the Next War."* Chicago: *Esquire,* 1935.

Mills, C. Wright. *The Sociological Imagination.* Oxford [England]: Oxford University Press, 2000.

Twenge, Jean M. *Generation Me: Why Today's Young Americans Are More Confident, Assertive, Entitled—and More Miserable Than Ever Before.* New York: Free Press, 2006.

Twenge, Jean M., and Campbell, Keith W. *The Narcissism Epidemic: Living in the Age of Entitlement.* New York: Free Press, 2010.

Acknowledgments

We would like to thank Scott Wright, René Blew, Jim Berlin, Bob Moore, Anne Luce, Jill Crandall, Doug Berlin, and Connie Pilato for their help. We also thank Casemate's Steve Smith, Tara Lichterman, and Libby Braden. And special thanks to John Zak of the *Dallas Morning News*.